Secrets from the Search Firm Files

Secrets from the Search Firm Files

What It Really Takes to Get Ahead in the Corporate Jungle

JOHN   RAU

With the senior partners of the Global
Search Firm of Ray and Berndtson

McGraw-Hill

New York   San Francisco   Washington, D.C.   Auckland   Bogotá
Caracas   Lisbon   London   Madrid   Mexico City   Milan
Montreal   New Delhi   San Juan   Singapore
Sydney   Tokyo   Toronto

Library of Congress Cataloging-in-Publication Data

Rau, John.
   Secrets from the search firm files : what it really takes to get
ahead in corporate America / John Rau.
     p. cm.
   Includes index.
   ISBN 0-7863-1192-4
    1. Executives—United States.   2. Chief executive officers—United
States.   3. Industrial management—United States.   4. Corporations—
United States.   I. Title.
HD38.25.U6R36   1997
658.4'.09–dc21   97–1469

McGraw-Hill

A Division of The McGraw·Hill Companies

1 2 3 4 5 6 7 8 9 0 DOC/DOC 9 0 9 8 7

ISBN 0-7863-1192-4

Printed and bound by R. R. Donnelley & Sons Company.

This publication is designed to provide accurate and
authoritative information in regard to the subject matter
covered. It is sold with the understanding that neither the
author nor the publisher is engaged in rendering legal, accounting,
or other professional service. If legal advice or other expert
assistance is required, the services of a competent professional
person should be sought.
    —*From a Declaration of Principles jointly adopted by a Committee
     of the American Bar Association and a Committee of Publishers.*

McGraw-Hill books are available at special quantity discounts to use as
premiums and sales promotions, or for use in corporate training programs.
For more information, please write to the Director of Special Sales,
McGraw-Hill, 11 West 19th Street, New York, NY 10011.
Or contact your local bookstore.

DEDICATION

This book is dedicated first to Michael, Caroline and Rebecca who were curious about the kind of book dad was writing and generally understanding when some editing at home cut short the games of "horse," "kings in the corner" or "concentration." Ultimately, however, it belongs to my wife Sandy who has helped me see that any limits or barriers to what you want to do are mostly the ones you have constructed yourself.

ACKNOWLEDGMENTS

This book never would have been possible without the enthusiasm and endorsement of Andy Olson and Linda Heagy, who started the ball rolling. And it never would have happened without the initiative and encouragement of my agent Jeremy Solomon. It never would have happened without Caroline Carney, the editor at McGraw-Hill, who got excited about an idea that was clearer in my head than perhaps it was in the early proposals. It never would have happened without Jeffrey Sund, of McGraw-Hill, who introduced the proposal. It certainly never would have happened without Sharon Voros, the director of communications at Ray and Berndtson, who saw the big picture from the beginning and helped the project get over a lot of the initial and complicated hurdles. It certainly never would have happened without Paul Ray, Jr., who not only endorsed the idea, but sponsored it with energy and conviction in a way that modeled and mirrored the enthusiasm that the rest of his partners brought to the project. And most of all, it would not have happened without the partners of Ray and Berndtson. They took a great deal of time away from their activities to reflect, to look through their files, to sort though the variety of factors and then to share graciously and selflessly their experiences, impressions, anecdotes and lessons with no other payoff than sharing what they know.

I also owe special thanks to Libby Andrew in the dean's office at the IU School of Business, who spent many hours transcribing, reassembling and proofreading drafts. I could always tell when she was transcribing one of my extra long sentences as her body became more and more motionless as she wanted for the end of a sentence that was long overdue in coming. I want to thank Diana Humphrey, my exceptional assistant, for helping Libby and me during the assembly process and for making everything else flow smoothly while keeping this project in perspective. I want to thank Mike Murray and the other partners I worked with at McKinsey for sharing their ideas and for the opportunity to compare notes with them on the work they did on high-performing organizations. And I want to thank Professors Janet Near and

Tim Baldwin, who helped me with some of the background on the search for managerial "magic bullets." I want to thank Dean Dan Dalton who did his usual magic in helping analyze the results of the survey part of our project and for his great insights on how to get the most out of this unique opportunity. I want to thank Kevin Thornton who served as "general contractor" and whose ideas for rearranging the pieces were exactly right. And I want to thank John McGauley, whose gifted ear and pen edited my drafts cleanly and sharply.

I offer appreciation and acknowledgment to three long-time colleagues. First to Joel Bleeke of McKinsey & Company; a long-time friend and fellow inquirer into why things work the way they do and how to help leaders think about their jobs. He also showed me what courage is all about. And I want to acknowledge Norm Bobins and Tom Heagy of LaSalle National Bank. As colleagues and partners for over a decade, they were responsible for pretty much everything we achieved together. Most important, they weren't reluctant to tell me clearly and candidly how I could improve as a manager and a CEO.

PREFACE

Why This Book?

Most managers eventually grow to understand that one of the most important things to do is help other managers develop. With your own success dependent upon the quality and motivation of those around you, there is no greater priority. I have always been intrigued by the question of what makes great managers. Which traits predict who has the potential to be great? To what degree are great leaders made, or born? Are they trainable? How do you spot them and sort the good from the bad?

My interest is anything but theoretical. I'm serving, for the third time, as the CEO of a relatively large company. Every CEO shares the same challenge. How do I evaluate my management talent? How do I pick the leaders of tomorrow? Which people should be developed and groomed to be the successor management team?

During the last decade, another dimension piqued my interest. American industry was in a revolution. People were changing jobs more quickly, careers were more volatile, and getting fired no longer meant that you had messed up. More people had to think about how to position themselves for mobility, especially with mergers and down-sizing becoming commonplace.

People started to talk about the same issues. "I am doing fine where I am, but I think it's time to get noticed." "Maybe I should make a move because circumstances where I am are probably not going to get any better." "How do I get my name on the map?" "How do I start playing this game of executive mobility?"

And they all say the same things: "I have had my head down, done a good job, worked hard, but I don't have a clue what to do to market myself."

Because I have friends in the executive search business and was used regularly as a source, I had some reasonable understanding of the process. And a search firm was involved in both of my last two moves.

As it turns out, my advice wasn't bad, but it was incomplete. I always wanted to write something more organized on this topic.

When I became Dean of the Indiana University School of Business, I had another reason to understand this "marketplace." Our faculty and I were responsible for designing curricula to help educate the managers of the future. We also had programs to help more senior executives enhance their careers. So it was key we understood what knowledge and characteristics the marketplace *really* required of people who will lead companies. Then the light bulb went on. What better place to get an objective read on what this marketplace does, in fact, require of executive talent than from the executive search firms who deal in this market everyday? Like the specialists on the stock exchanges, the partners of these global search firms are the specialists who "make" the market for executive talent.

So this book was born. A mass of unbiased data on what determines who gets included in searches and what determines who wins. The result, the *Secrets from the Search Firm Files*, is of value to anyone who is considering a job change. But even for those who are satisfied where they are, the lessons can only help.

The Lessons Work Even if You Never Move

Compared with the career patterns of the current generation of senior executives, fewer and fewer of today's rising executives will spend their entire career with a single company. So the requirements to understand and play the mobility game will apply to more and more people.

Not surprisingly, people who are successful in their current company are exactly those who will be the most attractive and successful candidates for outside opportunities. The underlying skills and practices are clearly the same.

What's less obvious is that the networking and visibility practices that put candidates on search firms' radar are beneficial within their current company. But when you think about it, it's clear that

- executives with outside options will always feel an advantage within their current employer;

- networking activities are *both* a source of learning and a way to communicate an executive's reputation for results;

- networking must be done when you don't expect to move, since it has almost no value if you start it only when it's clear you need to.

Finally, the secrets we uncovered about the issues of "cultural fit" are equally applicable to internal promotions. Most career "stall-outs" and voluntary resignations are due to lack of fit rather than major failures or lack of fundamental executive skills.

So while our data and perspective come from the movement of executives *between* companies, the lessons are equally useful regardless of how one expects his or her career to develop. It's taken me 25 years of leading organizations, selecting executives, and being on both sides of the executive search process to learn these secrets. No one who's serious about his or her own career can afford to ignore these rules of the executive marketplace.

ABOUT THE AUTHOR

John Rau, 48, is currently the President and Chief Executive Officer of Chicago Title and Trust Company, the country's largest title insurer and real estate services firm in the country, with 8,000 employees and revenue in excess of $1.5 billion annually. Its asset management units manage $10 billion.

Chicago Title is Rau's third Chief Executive Officer assignment. His first was when he was elected President of the Exchange National Bank of Chicago in 1983 at age 35. At the time, this made him the youngest CEO of any of the nation's top 100 banks. In 1989, Exchange National Bank was purchased by the ABN-AMRO group of the Netherlands (earning shareholders of Exchange National $42 million for each million invested at the start of his tenure), and he was asked to serve as the President and Chief Executive Officer of the LaSalle National Bank of Chicago, which was already owned by ABN-AMRO and which was merged with Exchange.

In 1993, he began a term as the dean of the School of Business at Indiana University. The IU School of Business is one of the nation's oldest and best management schools. Its undergraduate program is ranked as one of the five best in the country. Its MBA program was recently cited in *Business Week* as one of the five favorite schools for corporate recruiters looking for general managers, for marketing talent, and for finance graduates. The School of Business is 75 years old and has 66,000 living alumni around the world.

The board of directors of Chicago Title and Trust elected him as President and Chief Executive Officer in October 1996. A Harvard Business School graduate and the Goldman Sachs Finance Fellow at Harvard, Rau spent seven years with the First National Bank of Chicago before joining Exchange Bank. He has also worked as a special consultant to the firm of McKinsey and Company, studying the leadership traits of high-performing companies, and as a visiting scholar at Northwestern University's Kellogg Graduate School of Management. He and his wife Sandy (BS Dennison, MA, MBA Northwestern) and his children Michael, 14, Caroline, 12, and Rebecca, 8, live in the Chicago suburbs.

This book was written with the partners of the Global Executive Search Firm of Ray and Berndtson.

Ray and Berndtson is an executive search and management consulting firm with a network of 35 offices throughout the Americas, Europe, Asia and the Pacific Rim. One of the largest global executive search firms, Paul and Berndtson has more than 200 professionals in six U.S. cities, 14 European countries, Argentina, Australia, Canada, the People's Republic of China, Hong Kong, Japan and Mexico.

More than 65 percent of the firm's business comes from previous clients, which include industrial, financial and service companies, as well as government and not-for-profit organizations. Representative clients include

AT&T	*Ernst & Young*
Andersen Consulting	*Goodman, Sachs & Co.*
Banker's Trust Company	*Honeywell, Inc.*
Bell South Corporation	*Morgan Stanley & Co.*
Black & Decker	*Pfizer, Inc.*
Chase Manhattan Corp.	*Sara Lee Corporation*
Cigna Corporation	*Sumitomo Bank Ltd.*
ConAgra Inc.	*Tandy Corporation*
EDS	

Ray and Berndtson's top priority is providing executive search services of the highest possible quality. The firm's services include executive search, management audit and management consulting.

In addition to these primary services, the firm also conducts specialized consulting services for its clients. Some of these assignments have included compensation studies, market studies and assessments of joint venture partners or acquisition candidates.

CONTENTS

Chapter 3

The Semi-Finals: Getting on Search Firms' Radar   31

PART THREE

Tales from the Front: The Search Firm's Partners Speak   81

Chapter 7

What Search Firms' Partners Want to Know: If They Could Know Only One or Two Things about a Candidate   83

Chapter 8
The Worst Disaster I Ever Saw   87

Chapter 9
How to Be a Smart Client   93

PART FOUR

The Book of Lists   103

Chapter 10
Unspoken Assumptions: Evolution of the Mythic Manager   105

Chapter 11
The Early Years   115

Chapter 16
Afterwards   151

CHAPTER 1

Do as They Do; Not (Just) as They Say

When I was a business school dean, successful executives would visit my campus to give lectures and seminars. They also served as members of my Dean's Advisory Council. When asked by colleagues or students what they look for in people they hire, they echoed the same things. They want people who can think "strategically." They want people who can communicate clearly. They want people who can work well in teams, be positive motivators, with integrity, initiative and responsibility. They want people with an entrepreneurial attitude and a global perspective.

At the same time, their human resource directors and recruiters are hiring on criteria wildly different from what their bosses claim they want. Recruiters want expertise in a particular function. They want someone who can use the most current spreadsheet and computer modeling techniques. They would prefer someone who has had previous experience in the same industry, someone with an engineering or scientific background. And they want people who were raised in the same part of the country where the job is located.

What is going on here? Are the CEOs lying? Are they misinformed? Or have they just not bothered to talk with their own people?

The Real Rules

WHAT THE MIRROR DOESN'T SHOW

When CEOs talk there is a tendency for them to say the world would be better if everyone were just like themselves. So their speeches and observations on management reflect a self-image of which they are deservingly proud. Yet very few people really do become CEOs, and a world full of them might not necessarily be a better place. But they're not lying, nor are they misinformed.

CEOs and their HR executives are each describing only parts of a more complicated and interconnected reality. Some skills matter more and some less at various stages within a person's career. That's also true during the process by which a company and an individual evaluate each other and decide whether or not there is a good fit.

That's the basic premise of this book: most of what has been written about the characteristics of successful executives is true, but it is also only part of the story.

The well-known part of this story comes from those at the top, looking at their own reflections. They legitimately speak of standards and aspirations for their successors that will serve the company. But these skills take much time to develop. Meanwhile, there is a parallel process in which the market identifies, tracks, sorts and signals those executives who will advance. That process is not covered in these CEO speeches.

SURVEYS SAYS "SKILLS"; SCHOOLS TEACH THEORY

Several years ago, the Harvard Business School did a survey of its alumni, a high percentage of whom, of course, had gone on to become successful. The executives were asked to rank the various characteristics that determined success, and to place those characteristics as either long-term or short-term factors. Harvard recognized that these characteristics were likely to be different for young alums versus older graduates.

Surprisingly, while the factors shifted a little, the short- and long-term characteristics were consistent. More surprising, these lists were dominated by skills and attributes such as communications, analytic thinking, teamwork, integrity, and perseverance. Few of these were subjects taught explicitly at the Harvard Business School. And yet the school has a wonderful reputation as being the school that spawns the most CEOs, the school with the highest percentage who end up in the executive suite, and whose graduates are paid the most right out of school.

So what does that mean? Does it imply that the business school's principal function is to attract and sort people by these characteristics? Does it mean that these surveys are not complete? Unless you understand the rest of the real-world factors, and the issues of phasing and timing, it looks like a puzzle. Harvard has the highest starting salaries of any MBA program in the country. But is that because more of its graduates go directly into senior management? No. It is because a high percentage become investment bankers, money managers and consultants. The premium they are paid relates to raw intellectual capability and the flexibility to handle the variety of assignments that go with these professions. The premium also rewards the drive, energy and initiative required to work in these settings and the interpersonal skills and styles required to relate productively to client executives from day one. The premium also pays for the fact that most of the new recruits will wash out or quit long before they make partner.

THE JORDAN RULES AREN'T IN THE NBA RULEBOOK

So what's the rest of the story? How do you get in the game, stay in it, and position yourself for visibility and mobility at the right time and at the right stages?

Very few senior executives understand the rest of the story. They will, if prompted, acknowledge how they did a lot of the other things that it takes to be successful that we will talk about in this book. They understand the "real-world" rules, the randomness, the "missionary work" that is necessary for someone on this career track. They understand that one must be focused, deliberate, and well organized, not just visionary and inspiring, to have a broad set of career options. But these kinds of things are less fun to talk about. All of us want people to view the world in positive and noble terms, because that keeps us going as we encounter the boredom, drudgery, frustration and irritation that we all know is there, all the time.

That's why I responded to a "dare" to write a kind of "graduation speech" that no one ever really gives, because it deals with these kinds of "real rules" as well as the "big picture" principles that are the usual topics for these events.

The Graduation Speech You Will Never Hear

As a CEO, I have given a few commencement speeches. As a dean, you don't give many yourself, but you hear a lot more of them when you graduate bachelor's degrees, masters and doctoral students on multiple campuses.

Last week I pulled my cap and gown from the closet and dusted them off for another season—sort of like baseball cleats. Every year, a little fantasy of mine is to be sitting on a platform, listening as some dignitary violates all the sacred conventions of commencement speeches and tells all the students in the audience the realities of life. In this fantasy, the august speaker gives them a jolt of reality—rains on the parade in a big way. I chuckle each time I think about it, because it will never happen.

In the traditional graduation speech, the orator starts with something lofty like this: "With hard work everything is possible." In my fantasy speech he then adds, "But, of course, luck is really what we are talking about. Some very lazy people strike it rich. Being with the right company when it goes public will reward some of you slackers while many of you hard workers will be forced out with little to show after 15 or 20 years."

Then the speaker exhorts the audience to "find heroes and mentors" but adds this: "But, more times than not, you will be working for dopes with less talent than yourself. Your challenge will be to hold your tongue and get along until initiative, or luck, delivers you from ineptness." (Personally, I have never met a great executive who does not still remember the worst boss he or she ever had. Usually they can remember two or three.)

Graduation speeches exhort students to see everything as possible and to tap unbounded possibilities. But the world really tells you to have patience and wait your turn. Patience means understanding that the world does not exist to satisfy your career ambitions, but that your contributions to society are the quid pro quo for your needs to be considered. "And, graduates, remember this—it takes a long time for an organization to figure out it is you, and not the chairman's nephew, who is doing all the great work," the speaker says.

Graduation speeches stress thinking about the big picture, reaching out for breadth and diversity. But what the world really says is, tend to the here-and-now, focus on the local issues as defined by your boss and job. The real world says you had better prove reliable to your colleagues in the little details before you get to play with the bigger toys and resources in an organization.

The speaker invokes the brotherhood of mankind and our solidarity as humans. But in the fantasy, this speaker says: "You are going to run into plenty of people who will not like you, and there is damn little you can do about it. Sure, there is bigotry based on gender, color or religion, but they also will not like you for other equally irrational reasons—you just do something that irritates them." (Or you remind them of someone who jilted or insulted them.) But it may be a while before I hear a speaker exhort graduates to ignore this inevitability as much as possible and say, "The fight is frequently not worth it, and the opponent is usually not worth the effort anyway. Live with it."

The rest of the fanstasy speech continues in the same vein. On the left, I've put the traditional cliché. On the right, the reality rules.

Cliché	Reality Rule
"Speak the truth, hold strong against all temptations to prevaricate and make no moral compromises."	"In the real world you do not talk in elevators, you do not criticize the organization except in subtle and acceptable ways, you do not demand that organizations take on the responsibility for solving all the world's problems. Your obligation for honesty is for major and moral issues, not what you truly think of the boss's recent brainstorm."
"Seek beauty and ennoblement in the arts, in literature, in poetry, dance, painting and music."	"You had better find most of your beauty and ennoblement in the more commonplace arts like driving a car pool, coaching Little League and serving snacks as room parent. For most of us, our primary artistry will show, if at all, only after our children turn 25 and begin to discover, to their amazement, that their parents not only had good judgement but actually contributed positively to their own development and character."

Cliché	Reality Rule
"Accept and relish the challenge of change. Our world will be unrecognizable in a few decades and you the graduate will play a critical role in bringing on the new millennium."	"People hate change—and with good reason. Lots of changes are hardly for the better (tell me again why we deregulated phone service). The key is having the judgment to figure out <u>which</u> changes are good for you."

So, when you put it altogether, what does this real-world commencement speech sound like? Well, you would come away with the following notes on a pad:

Cliché	Reality Rule
"Work hard."	"Do not be too surprised if someone else gets luckier."
"Reach for nobility and love of mankind."	"Do not feel you have to convert every bigot or snob. Pick your friends and pick your fights and save your strength for the battles over your most basic values."
"Learn from great minds and seek challenging situations."	"Do not be discouraged when you end up working for a series of dopes. You will learn more from those who screw up than by copying the relative few who are magnificent role models."
"Value honesty above all."	"Do not feel the need to share the unvarnished truth at every single moment."
"Do not be afraid to think of things as they should be."	"Understand that there are thousands of reasons and thousands of years behind why things are the way the are."
"It is important you make your mark on the world."	"Start by making sure your own children have at least the same benefits and values you were given."

This fantasy speech appeared in a slightly different form in the <u>Atlanta Constitution</u> on March 11, 1996.

There's one thing that makes me sure that this is the graduation speech you will never actually hear. That's because it sounds too much like what your parents have told you for years. And no matter how true, great speakers know that 18-year-olds do not cheer for something they have heard so many times before.

But on behalf of parents and those who have seen it all play out this way, wouldn't it be fun just once to have someone in a cap and gown tell it like it is? We all know the reasons why not, of course. Graduates learn it soon enough and our job during commencement is to give them reasons to jump out of the academic nest and take on the real world, even when the real world may greet them more with a shrug than a cheer.

When I wrote this book, it was clearly with tongue in cheek. But it does suggest that, much as there is an insider's view of success that should be grounded in the details, so too is there an insider's view of the workings of the market for senior executives that has lessons for all of us. These are the practical (and irrational) realities that the professionals understand. These are the secrets of the search firm files. And these are the lessons all executives who make it to the top understand.

Extracting the Secrets

How We Learned the Lessons

The methodology we used was straightforward. We created a study instrument that started with the skills, experiences, personality types and career paths that make up a senior executive's profile. We looked for variables and patterns that brought people to the attention of a search firm, the characteristics most likely to make an executive the winning candidate, and the attributes that were most important to the success of top executives. We looked at which traits were fixable, and at which skills and traits held people back, but were ultimately correctable. We looked, too, for fatal flaws, characteristics that knocked people out of the running for good.

We had access to the files on all the searches that Ray and Berndtson did in the last two-and-one-half years, and selected a broad sample of 78 senior management positions as the basis of our study. The 30 partners who handled these searches filled out our surveys. I also conducted extensive interviews with each partner to gather a full perspective. *Secrets from the Search Firm Files* is not conjecture.

We did not guess at which qualities people looked for in hiring executives, nor did we rely on opinions of executives as to why they were successful. We had the actual "spec sheets" that are used to guide each search. Nor did we have to guess which traits gave certain individuals the specific opportunity to consider offers for mobility and advancement. We also had the "presentation" reports the search executives used in helping the hiring firm winnow down to the final candidates.

Best of all, we had the perspective of people who, collectively, have handled more than 5,000 searches during the last 20 years.

THE DATA IN OUR DATABASE

The 78 senior management searches whose files were part of this study were for strategic business unit heads, subsidiary presidents, sector executives, senior corporate officers and chief executive officers. We did not include searches for technical positions or corporate staff positions. We excluded positions where expertise in one topic, rather than leadership skill and potential for advancement into general management, was the most important characteristic. Table 1.1 shows the distribution of these searches in our sample by job type. The compensation levels ranged from the low- and mid- six figures to totals well in seven figures. We

TABLE 1.1   Job Title Distribution

Title	Number	Percent
Chairman, CEO or president & CEO	15	19.2
President and/or chief operating officer	28	36.0
Division or subsidiary president	4	5.1
Executive in charge of marketing, manufacturing or line(s) of business	11	14.1
Corporate officer EVP, SVP, VP	11	14.1
Other senior	9	11.5
Total	78	100.0

excluded searches where a language skill or a particular cultural back‐ground (i.e., for a particular overseas posting) was a dominant charac‐teristic because these searches tended to have different sorting characteristics.

The data in the tables in Chapters 2, 3 and 4 reflect a very high response rate from the partners. In only a handful of cases (less than 10) did we conclude we couldn't obtain data that was sufficiently compa‐rable and dependable to be included in the final tabulations. In essen‐tially all these cases, this was because someone involved in the search was no longer with the firm. In a few cases, the research consultant had left and it was not clear enough from the records how all the initial candidates were discovered. In a few cases, we had the specs and the presentation reports but the partner who knew why the finalist was selected was not available. So while all the currently active partners contributed to the open‐ended questions, the priority ranking of fac‐tors reflects 85–90% of the sample, depending upon the category.

LIMITATIONS AND CAVEATS

Our study sample was big enough to reasonably draw conclusions that the patterns we saw are likely to occur in a very high percentage of other similar searches. So the broad lessons are both reliable and, to people familiar with the process, not too surprising. What no survey can tell us, of course, is how personal "chemistry" and fit affect a par‐ticular search, and those obviously affect searches to a high degree. There are candidates with all the right background and all the right profile who just do not ignite a spark with either the search consultant or the client even though on paper they look like perfect candidates. Similarly, we cannot categorically say that unless you have these char‐acteristics and patterns, you cannot get in the game. People get hired on hunches, intuition, or a gut sense that someone's experience in a dif‐ferent area will translate well.

The point is, the rules are not hard and fast and there are exceptions. The biggest caveat of all is that you have to combine the profile with spe‐cific opportunities. A .300 hitter sitting on the bench will not get any hits, while a relief pitcher at least has a practical chance of a home run when he is at the plate. So getting a chance to swing at big league pitches is an important skill. But once you get this chance you had better know how to hit for average, how to hit for scoring and how to hit as part of an offense. But somebody first has to put your name on a lineup card.

Successful executives are made and not born. Family background, family social or economic status, attending the "right" schools are anything but determinative. In fact, the most common shaping experiences for successful senior executives are not the most distinguished families or the most affluent backgrounds, or the most prestigious schools, but those settings where struggles and testing and lack of "predetermination" are present.

In other words, anybody *can* do it. And people from essentially every kind of background *have* done it. However, very few *will* do it, because the odds are low, the work is hard, and the risks are high. But it is clear that those who understand this game, those that understand the imperatives of this food chain, are the ones who end up with the best chance of ending up near its top.

THE VIEW FROM THE TOP

Every food chain has a top and a bottom. What is unique about studying the top is that one can learn a great deal about the dynamics of the entire chain. This is *not* equally true at the bottom, or even in the middle. By studying the "dominating" capabilities of persons at the top, we learn something about what the other members of the chain must be like. We can also study characteristics that prevent top people from being dominated. This too tells us a great deal about the characteristics and limitations of those below.

The global market for senior executives is, basically, a food chain. It is driven by the inexorable pressures of corporate evolution and the Darwinian dynamic of survival of the fittest. Each year, hundreds of thousands of business school graduates, MBAs, management trainees, entrepreneurs and technical professionals enter the first rung of the managerial food chain and begin a long, slow climb. Many are ejected, more stall out, and only a few enter that magic echelon where they can pick among an unlimited number of senior jobs. These select few can move out and up whenever they are frustrated or seek new challenges. The global search firms keep track of them, keep in touch with them and promote their achievements and reputations to potential employers. That is why studying those executives who move from one senior job to another is such a good way to learn about the skills that make for executive success. It is this premise that is at the heart of the *Secrets from the Search Firm Files*.

PART ONE

Three Steps to the Executive Suite

The process of climbing to a new executive position involves three discrete steps:

1. Matching the "specs" of the search that the new company is conducting. This means having the background, experiences and skills that fit the job requirements.

2. Getting noticed or discovered by the search firm handling the assignment.

3. Outscoring the other candidates who have succeeded in stages one and two.

What is less obvious is that the rules are different for each of these three stages. So are the skills, background and activities that separate the successful from the less successful players at each stage.

This section presents the results of our survey. You will see the pattern of how some of these factors are constant for all three stages, and how others shift up and down in relative importance.

In Chapter 2, we describe the specifications that the client firms established. We address two key dimensions: Why is that key element of the job specification so important, and how do executives develop those skills? We will talk about typical experiences, and the drills and practices that executives who have these skills tend to follow.

In the next chapter, "The Semi-Finals," we focus on attracting the attention of the search firms. We also talk about these same key executive characteristics, how some are more important and others less; but we focus on *how* individuals show that they have these experiences. Also, how do search firms discover who has these personal skills and backgrounds? We talk about how the search firms decide how much credibility to give to each of these characteristics when interviewing candidates.

In the third chapter in this section (Chapter 4), "The Finals," we talk about the same characteristics with the focus on how the client firms judge who has the necessary traits. We look at how search firms and client companies assess what is the least scientific, but most important, factor in the competition for top jobs. This is the elusive notion of "cultural fit."

Chapter 2

The Quarterfinals: What All Clients Want

The Primary Specifications for General Management

Priority One—History of Demonstrated Results

Table 2.1 breaks out the relative ranking of the top five factors that showed up on clients' specifications for this sample of general management positions.

TABLE 2.1 Top Five Factors on Client Specifications for Senior Management Searches

Factor	% Very High	Rank	% High or Very High
Reputation for results	81.03	1	94.83
Ability to think strategically	75.86	2*	89.66
Communication skills	75.86	2*	96.55
Fit with company culture	74.14	4	84.48
Interpersonal skills	72.41	5	98.28

*Tied for second place.

Not surprisingly, client spec sheets reflect many of the same pro-files that CEOs tell us are the most important factors for general management. Leading the list is a reputation for having achieved results. The best predictor of success is past successes. Paper routes and school leadership activities predict early job success. Success in early jobs predicts success in bigger jobs. So it is not surprising that the number one priority that companies state is to find someone who has achieved results in other places. *In fact, this reputation for results is the one factor that does not change in relative importance across the three stages of a search.* Both the clients and the search firms understand that no interview techniques, resume, style, charisma or personal skill can be as good a predictor of success as someone who has been successful.

This is all obvious, but what is important in stages two and three is understanding that it is difficult to determine how much of a company's success is appropriately attributed to an individual candidate. Search firm partners say the one thing that they want to know is a candidate's *real* contributions to a success. As one of them put it, "I would like to understand exactly where his or her fingerprints were on what happened."

This is the foundation for two initial lessons: "upside" and "down-side." The upside rule is *work your way into circumstances where it is unambiguously clear what your contribution is, what you are responsible for and how it can be measured.* For example, if you are the president of a subsidiary that is measured as a separate P&L and you had three or four years of sales and profit, then it's going to be a lot easier to find your fingerprints on the success than if you were the corporate marketing officer whose role in the volume-building of a new brand is hard to calibrate.

The downside rule is *never* overstate or imply a greater link between yourself and the results of a company than is unarguably the case. This is a critical factor—one that was mentioned by *every* search consultant. *The easiest ways to shoot yourself in the foot as a candidate is to inflate your role in past successes.*

There is nothing more embarrassing to a search consultant than to put forth a candidate who is found to have overstated his or her record.

Priority Two—Ability to Think Strategically

The second most important item clients place on spec sheets is the ability to think strategically. That is what general managers are paid to do; that and to motivate people to implement the strategy. (Which is why interpersonal and communication skills are two of the next three most important factors.) But what does this mean? And how do you develop this skill to think strategically?

People in leadership roles, people who have achieved success, have in fact looked out over the horizon and pictured the world as it *could* be. Only then did they take the steps to communicate that vision to others and shape the organization to fit that picture. At this strategic level the stakes are the highest, the time frames longest, and the risks most substantial. Those who see the opportunities, and threats, can picture the successful path and move an organization in that direction create the most value.

The question is, where do you get this skill and how do you recognize it in others? One of the best drills to develop strategic thinking is to study history. Great generals, great politicians and even great athletes have studied not only the most successful practitioners of their art, but all of the classic encounters. Through these studies of history they understand the kinds of options available to leaders and the interactions that occur in a competitive situation. They understand the dynamics of a "strategic challenge."

Strategic thinkers also have a broad understanding of the external forces that come to bear on a company. They are consumers not only of history, but of news. They want to understand the fundamental models of economics and politics, of production and engineering, of science and technology. Strategic thinkers always want to know, "How does it work?" Early in their careers they develop the habit of studying the strategic decisions of the companies they are in. They ask themselves, "Why did these decisions get made, how were they made, would I have done the same thing?"

How do you tell if someone has this ability? In the best case, you can isolate specific circumstances where the candidate has, in fact, been responsible for a strategic shift and its implementation. But even an experienced executive might be able to point to only one or two such clear-cut cases. As a result, search consultants develop a "sense" of how well someone thinks strategically, not by just listening to how candidates describe circumstances *they* were in or what *they* did, but by the nature of the questions they ask about the company and its circumstance. If the questions are about the competition, the environment, the alternatives, the risks and the resources, they impart a strong sense of thinking strategically. A candidate who talks about the internal procedures, mechanics of the job, reporting relationships and budgeting procedures illustrates only tactical thinking. Tactical issues are important, but the most successful individuals are those who first study a situation and assess the general competitive situation and where change can be made. Good leaders focus on the big strategic issues because that is what interests them. Those people assume that procedures and tactics be changed to complement the strategic mission.

It is not surprising that at the top of every spec sheet are two things: a reputation for results and the ability to think strategically. Equally rational is the item that shows up tied for second place, communication skills.

Priority Three—Communication Skills

Every manager knows there is only one tool to move an organization in a strategic direction—effective and convincing communication.

Communication skills are vital because they are the only link between strategy and action. It doesn't matter how smart you are or how right you are, if the rest of the people either don't understand what it is you want or think they do understand but have something different in mind, you have failed as a leader.

Managerial jobs require more and more good judgment. Hierarchies are being flattened so that one's superior does not hand out tasks minute by minute. And with companies operating around the clock and around the globe, there isn't the time to wait until it is clear everyone is doing exactly what is required. So it is vital that people *understand* what is expected of them.

They need to not only understand, but to accept. Today people no longer accept as a given that they should automatically do whatever it is that the company tells them to do. They have been brought up to understand that they have the right to understand *why* something is going to be done. They believe that they have the *right to judge* the rightness of a policy. They believe they have the right to question leaders, and the right to personal involvement in the decision-making process. Against this background it is no wonder that senior executives are not only judged by, but totally reliant on, communication skills to persuade, convince and lead.

There have been countless studies about productivity in organizations. It turns out that employees' feelings about management's explanations of the company's future are one of the highest predictors of productivity and worker motivation. The better "connected" they feel to management's agenda, the more positive they become.

In his book, *Work and the Nature of Man,* Frederick Herzberg wrote that it was *not* working conditions, pay, company policies and so on that determine whether people were satisfied and productive. He asserted that "intrinsic" factors, that is, the sense of challenge, the sense of participation in something useful, the sense of identification with the company and its goals, determined how satisfied (and productive) people were.

Since that book was written, time has proven him right. This makes clear just how vital communication skills are to the senior executive. They are the *only* weapon he or she has to engage the organization on terms that are likely to make it the most effective and productive over the long haul.

This is not to say that inarticulate, monosyllabic or "grammatically challenged" executives cannot succeed. But it makes the job more difficult and the odds against success more substantial. Just compare the last two Republican presidents. Ronald Reagan was "the great communicator," highly effective as a leader, engaging Americans in a nearly revolutionary change in government strategy that politicians with greater intellect or greater experience could not accomplish.

The contrast with George Bush was stark. He lacked Reagan's gifts for making points clearly at a level that the audience was most likely to respond to. Bush was a man with a wonderful reputation of public service. He engineered one of the most significant foreign policy victories imaginable by assembling a difficult coalition during Desert Storm. Yet he was turned out of office less than two years later because he was unable to communicate his affection for the country and his sense of priorities. He admitted he had trouble with "the vision thing." Unfortunately, "the vision thing" is a codeword for making people feel engaged and motivated. That weakness is a fatal flaw in a leader.

Is a good communicator born or trained? Of all executive skills, this talent can be developed with focus, practice and perseverance. I recommend a three-ingredient recipe to become a good communicator. First, develop a vocabulary that allows you to express a broad range of ideas with nuance. If you are limited by the same short list of verbs and adjectives, it is like being a cook who only has a handful of ingredients. The more ingredients you have in your cupboard and the fresher and stronger they are, the more variety and excitement there will be to the dishes you create.

Learning vocabulary is a function of doing a large amount of reading and in a variety of fields. Read literature to see how good writers have used words to describe, to convey setting, to convey image and to convey emotion. A diet of business books, spy novels and the sports pages won't do much for your vocabulary. (With this book being an exception.) The good communicator leavens this basic diet with good doses of the classics, novels and dramas that focus on the human condition and convey setting and background. Opinion magazines and literary/editorial journals use language to strongly argue points of view. Regardless of your own political leanings, read the opinion magazines from the other side of the aisle. Reading things that you agree with doesn't stimulate your brain as much as things that challenge your beliefs. Next down the food chain are the great newspapers and magazines, whose writing is far preferable to that of most metropolitan dailies.

SEARCH FIRM SECRETS

How to Become a Great Communicator

✓ Stretch your vocabulary; read widely.

✓ Read classics and drama which convey emotion.

✓ Read opinion journals which argue points of view.

✓ Be brief and edit down intensely.

✓ Engage the human side.

✓ Talk up to your audience but in plain words.

The second ingredient is to be focused, brief, direct, and to engage the most human parts of the audience. Memos should be brief, with the conclusion and required or suggested action in the first paragraph. Supporting facts and rationale must be contained within two or three pages. Larger "broadcast" memos should assume that people are literate adults who do not need to be protected from clarity on subjects they may not like or agree with.

Many executives, whether it is in front of groups, in memos or in meetings, feel that they need to be ponderous and grave. They rarely use short words or talk as human beings do. They feel they need to be dry or emotionless, draining human feelings from corporate governance. All these styles inhibit effective communication. People understand that management has both the right and the obligation to take action and enforce practices that people may resist. But as long as the policies are for the good of the organization, they will go along. What people resent is being addressed as children or being manipulated by double talk. Compare the following examples and decide which is more likely to diminish the credibility of management.

MEMO ONE

To: Staff

Subject: Company Cars

As you know, we are having a very tough year financially. Except for those whose jobs involve more than 20,000 driving travel miles a year, we are eliminating company cars for everybody else. Right now this is a perk we cannot afford. We are sorry, and I am sure we all hope that we can reopen this topic at some time in the future.

MEMO TWO

To: Staff

Subject: Re-evaluation of Private Transportation Expense Alternatives

A procedure has been set-up whereby private ground transportation expenses and alternative delivery modes for all employees entitled to use company resources for ground transportation need to be re-evaluated in light of current fiscal considerations. Employees who currently have ground transportation resources or dedicated vehicles at their disposal will be expected to

```
submit a justification of the rational for
continued provision thereof. It is expected that
those individuals whose current documentable
utilization of company-provided transportation
exceeds 5,000 miles per calendar quarter will be
assumed to have an acceptable rationale for
continued provision of ground transportation. All
others should expect that, in the absence of
extraordinary contrary factors, for the duration
of the current period of financial dislocation,
the company will not subsidize and/or directly
provide ground transportation resources.
```

Ingredient three is practice, practice, practice. No one ever became a world-record long distance runner merely by wanting to and no one ever became a great communicator without taking every opportunity to practice. Practice eliminates nervousness and develops a relaxed, mature and self-confident style. Only actual presentations help someone to get comfortable with pacing, with making connection with the audience, with working with both scripts and outlines, and with handling questions.

Some firms employ communication consultants who can be excellent critical observers to help improve your skills. Use videotape to see how you look in front of an audience. Just as important is editing memos. Most should be edited several times before sending. There is nothing worse than an incomprehensible memo. It is not just a failure to communicate, it's an indication of the writer's executive ability. Have others look at drafts and give you back in two or three sentences what it meant. Ask readers if your drafts do what they feel they are expected to do and how it made them feel. Edit your work with emphasis on clarity rather than trying to impress them with how much work you have done.

The most common complaint from senior executives about newly minted MBAs is they cannot write well. They don't write concisely or appreciate the reader's point of view. Perhaps the most common of these new MBA communication sins is the desire to show the reader how much work they did. Business memos should not be written like murder mysteries, that is, the goal is *not* to keep the reader in suspense until the last paragraph and then have the reader say, "Aha, that's how it all fits together." The chairman of the board of the first company at which I worked had a great rule for all young MBAs. He insisted that any memo written to him be two pages or less in total length. Within the first two paragraphs, the action he was expected to take, the conclusion he was expected to reach, or the fact he was suppose to learn had to be expressed in one *underlined* sentence. And yet every year, young executives send thirty or fifty page memos to their superiors assuming they can be impressed by the total heft of the document.

Unfortunately, the widespread adoption of e-mail has worsened this problem. It is too easy to crank out junk on your computer and send it without doing any editing. Remember, the goal is *not* to take advantage of *your* time by composing something quickly. The goal *is* to use the time of your readers wisely; to make sure they understand what they are supposed to do. If you ask someone to read something irrelevant or unimportant, you have imposed a cost on the organization far larger than the extra ten minutes it would take you to edit your own work and to think through who should get it and why.

Priority Four—Fit with Company Culture

The first three specifications all mean the same thing for every company and executive position. A "cultural fit" means quite different things for each company, and is not something you can prepare for in a generic way. In Chapter 6 we will talk more about "fit" and how recruiters decide who "fits" with a particular company.

There is no question that "fit" is a key item. But "fit" does not mean conformity. Fit means you have the skills and style the company needs at that time. It means you have a compatible orientation toward decision-making and how people work together. It means you have values that make it likely you will be able to work with others in senior management. It means you bring to the table the "missing ingredient" that a company needs to face new challenges or to move in new directions.

It's obvious that every executive will not fit every culture. Fit is not a mark of success or failure, but if the fit isn't natural, a "forced fit" never works. Clients that pretend to have a company culture different than what it is will end up seeing managers leave when they discover the truth. Similarly, candidates who pretend to be what the company wants, as opposed to what they are, will either become frustrated or disenchanted, but will certainly not be productive or contribute to the company's success. The elements of cultural fit are diverse. They include traits like degree of aggressiveness, decision-making style, and whether a company is "upward" looking, "outward" looking, tolerant of eclectic interests or insistent that people share the same values and lifestyles. Culture includes factors such as whether a company is change-oriented, or in crisis, or fast-paced, or stable.

The elements of fit are a function of the individual's own upbringing and previous experiences. For example, candidates are presumed to have adopted the culture of the places they have worked. Therefore, one important piece of advice: it helps to have spent some time at what search consultants call "academy companies," well-known firms perceived to have positive, energetic cultures, and to be aggressive, challenging and discriminating in their hiring. Household names like Motorola, McKinsey, Pepsi, Microsoft, the U.S. Marines and West Point are all examples of organizations that have a clear public cultural persona which will reflect well upon people who spend time at them.

While there is great variability in the specifics of a company's culture, an essential ingredient of cultural fit everywhere is the ability to get along with people. Which is why priority number five is as high as it is.

Priority Five—Interpersonal Skills

The inclusion of interpersonal skills as one of the top five executive traits is consistent in any survey of executives. It is also one of the most fuzzy criteria and one that raises the most questions among both MBA students and middle managers. They cannot understand what this means or why is it important. "If I am doing my job and I know what I am doing, what does it matter if I am a social butterfly?" A senior manager will say, "I am not running a popularity contest; my goal is for the company to be successful. I'm not going to waste a lot of time trying to charm employees or pretend that this place is some kind of democracy when it clearly isn't."

All these protestations miss the mark. People skills are not about being nice, friendly in a phony way, or pretending that the workplace is something it isn't. People skills involve understanding that people have choices and their productivity is a function of their attitude and respect for the people with whom they work. The single best predictor of peoples' attitudes toward their company is their relationship with their supervisor. If they respect that person and feel respected in return then you have the most positive kind of environment. *Having people skills means having the understanding and instinct to treat people as you yourself would like to be treated.*

People skills allow companies to adapt to today's rapid change. To be able to employ multifunctional teams, or teams between company suppliers and customers, top executives must set the example of being respectful, yet open, friendly yet professional, courteous and polite yet efficient in their use of time. Successful leaders learn to handle disagreements without having them become personal.

MBAs often ask about how to develop people skills. My advice is to spend more time with people, be open to others and allow that experience to affect you. You learn how effective groups operate when you focus on helping others. I suggest that, instead of relying on your strengths to be less dependent on people, you make yourself vulnerable to and committed to other groups, to understand what people need from leadership.

Ironically, to lead is to understand that the role of the leader is to serve. Your job is to make the people who work for you more productive, rather than having them serve you. You must learn to listen and not talk, to take criticism without defense. Good leaders don't argue, but deal with the source of the misperception. The don't blame people or accuse them for coming to the

SEARCH FIRM SECRETS

When They Say "Good People Skills," What Do They Mean?

- ✓ Look through others' eyes.
- ✓ Treat people like you want to be treated.
- ✓ Be respectful but open.
- ✓ Assume good will and good intentions.
- ✓ Use others' time efficiently.
- ✓ Give honest feedback on behaviors.
- ✓ Keep an open mind.

wrong conclusion. Leaders with good people skills assume good will; they pay attention to others and seek feedback. They take it as their responsibility to ensure that appropriate conclusions are reached.

People with good skills treat junior subordinates and nonmanagerial staff not as computers but as individuals. You learn their names and have short but polite conversations with them. Visit people on their own turf and don't assume that your exalted position in the hierarchy should make everyone come to you. Show respect for their time and interest in their activities. People want to feel good about themselves and they want other people to feel good about themselves. They want to feel trusted, respected and enthusiastic. They want to feel interested and they want to feel valued. So all you really need to do is find out from the people you work with how you make *them* feel.

Unlike communications skills, improving people skills does not require outside consultants. Everyone you work with has a good read on your interpersonal skills, and knows how, and where, you can improve. The trick is being open to receiving feedback. This requires you to feel capable of accepting it and others to feel trusting enough to give it without fear or concern. As you become better and better at placing yourself in other's shoes, you will learn more and more. We are all so focused on our own activities and our own feelings that it is hard to get that "outside-in" perspective. As you acquire the habit of "automatic empathy," your people skills will grow. People who hire top executives put people skills among their top five necessary traits. They know that people who don't know how to get along, or are self-centered, will ultimately fail, since no one will be following where they are trying to lead.

Priority Six—Reputation for Organizational Building

This was a very high factor in position specifications, with more than 80 percent of recruiters listing it high or very high (see Table 2.2). It is similar to the reputation for results. But it refers to the ability to change and improve an organization, not just wringing results from an existing firm. Companies that are stable, not having problems, and satisfied with the status quo, are more likely to have an internal candidate. They look to someone who "grew up in the culture" to continue it on its course. But when a company is looking for a senior executive from the outside, there is a perceived need to change strategy or to deal with new challenges. Dissatisfaction with the status quo drives many searches. Therefore, the ability to "grow" the organization in the face of threats is key.

Today, this element becomes more and more important. Every firm, including even the most traditionally strong companies, recognizes the need to build, continuously improve and face new challenges and opportunities. The most visible example of this is the recruitment of Lou Gerstner to IBM. IBM symbolized a most extraordinary shift in American industry. Its leadership came from within. The troubles they encountered made it clear anyone can get into trouble. What they needed was someone with a reputation for organizational change and leadership to challenge the established traditions that got them into trouble. Gerstner's reputation as a builder was developed at American Express and solidified with how he handled the extraordinary challenges at RJR Nabisco. He also was qualified as a strategic thinker, a good communicator, had a reputation for results and had good people skills. But the IBM board's willingness to take on someone who didn't know the industry was due to his reputation for effecting major change.

TABLE 2.2 Client Specifications for Senior Management Searches, Factors Six through Ten

Factor	% Very High	Rank	% High or Very High
Reputation for organizational building	65.52	6	81.03
Previous comparable position	63.79	7*	91.38
Previous P&L (line management) experience	63.79	7*	77.59
Previous industry experience	50.00	9	77.59
Sales and marketing experience	48.28	10	79.31

*Tied for seventh place.

Priorities Seven through Nine—Previous Comparable Position, Previous P&L or Line Management Experience, Previous Industry Experience

Comparable positions and previous line experience were rated as very high by slightly over 60 percent of the sample. Previous industry experience was rated very high in about half. It's clear that at senior levels there is an understanding someone must have been in a comparable senior position, preferably with line responsibilities for P&L, but not necessarily in the same industry.

Specific industry experience doesn't carry nearly as much weight as P&L responsibility. It was still listed as a very important factor in half the searches, but in two-thirds of the cases the requirement is more accurately stated as having previously *comparable* line experience. The rare case will be the person who has achieved relatively senior positions mostly through staff jobs, yet who is still viewed as a candidate for these senior executive jobs. But "cross-functional" promotions are much more likely within a company than via a search. At senior levels, you can change from line to staff, or get promoted, but it's hard to do both in one move.

The lessons are obvious. Your track record is viewed as clearly applicable within your own industry, and is also strongly applicable in comparable kinds of positions. The ability to cross industry lines or industry segment lines is relatively easy. What is more difficult is to attract these kinds of opportunities without the reputation for results and a history of success in handling the challenges of building organizations during periods of threat and/or opportunity.

It is less important that you position yourself in a particular industry than it is to build an individual track record that you can point to as proof you "satisfy" each of these top eight or nine factors. For senior positions it is essential that you earn "check marks" in *all* of these top eight or nine factors. It will be only the rare case where someone will be considered without meeting all these high priority qualifications. People don't advance in this game with "voids" in their profile.

Our studies indicated that, while still relatively substantial percentages list factors ten through sixteen as being high or very high, these are also the "wish list." These are the "nice," but not necessary, aspects. These factors broaden your appeal, but are not necessarily fatal if you lack them. I would include both sales and marketing experience in the top ten and at the top of this next group. Whether these are "vital" or just "useful" skills is a function of the job and the company culture. Everyone recognizes that business leaders benefit from having experience on the customer side and in actually generating revenue. But a heavy sales career is also viewed as a bit of a two-edged sword. Sales and marketing executives are viewed as having limited abilities in strategic thinking. The caricature is that they have personalities that are too short-term oriented.

Some companies have a bias toward the financial, strategic or the operational/engineering profiles for their chief executive positions. If your career has developed primarily or exclusively on the sales and marketing side, you may be viewed as a less attractive candidate than someone with a diversity of experience. Again, each company is different, but as a general career rule it is important to demonstrate results in each of the major functions. One fundamental question executives should ask themselves is if they can do this within a single company or if they need to look for outside opportunities to create the balanced profile for a broader variety of senior management roles.

Priority group three is the list of "useful" specifications for senior management positions. These are desirable, but not absolutely required. We have already discussed sales and marketing experience as being both

TABLE 2.3 Priority Group Three

Factor	% Very High	Rank	% High or Very High
Sales and marketing	48.28	10	79.31
Charm and charisma	41.38	11	65.52
Physical appearance	25.86	12*	60.34
Background in specific technology	25.86	12*	53.45
Advanced degree	24.14	14	60.34
International experience	18.97	15	48.28
Prestigious education	17.24	16	31.03

*Tied for twelfth place.

the bottom of the top ten and the first one that is typically on the "nice to have" section. Note that sales and marketing experience is essentially the last factor where the sum of both the very high and high ratings put it close to 80 percent.

Number 11 on the list is "charm and charisma" with 40 percent rating it very high. I was surprised by this, as were a number of the partners. They felt than since we asked about charm and charisma together, it shows up because typically a description of a desirable executive is a strong leader with charismatic qualities and good interpersonal skills. So to some degree it is a reflection of the fact that people understand that successful leaders have charisma. But both the search firms and the clients are aware of the distinction between charming yet ineffective people and those for whom that is just another attribute of results.

Physical appearance is factor 12. There is no question that, all things being equal, there is an advantage to being conventionally good-looking, well-groomed, in shape, and attractive. It is not so much that people are looking for physical attractiveness as they understand that people who take pride in their appearance and show self-discipline bring the same traits to their work. There is no automatic correlation between skill and appearance. But in our culture tall is better than short, thin is better than fat, attractive is better than homely.

Factor number 13 on the list is background in the specific technology. This is not a dominant factor in most cases. There are companies which believe individuals need some familiarity with their key technology, while others believe management skills transcend the background. All things being equal, recruiters would prefer some exposure to engineering, technology or physical science, biological science, computers, marketing technology, consumer products, or whatever is at the "core" of the company. But they interpret technology in the broadest sense. Again, the key lesson is that it is not so much the technology or the specific industry that defines your profile as an executive. It *is* whether you have achieved a reputation for results and can demonstrate the key skills of senior executives.

Factor 14 is having an advanced degree. As former dean of one of the country's better business schools, readers might think I find it discouraging that such a relatively low percentage feel that an MBA is necessary. Only a quarter said an advanced degree was important, and even fewer think it is important that it come from a prestigious school

(18%) (factor 16). It is not that I don't think advanced degrees and especially ones from the better schools create advantages. But factors rank low because the half-life of these advantages is short. MBAs from good schools allow people to be more competitive immediately after graduation. And there is a greater range of job opportunities presented to graduates of better schools for their *first* job. But by the time people are candidates for general management, it is presumed that the benefits of their education will have shown up in their work.

Factor 15 involves international experience. It came as a surprise to me that, with all of the focus on the globalization of industry, only half listed international experience as an important factor. In almost all cases, an understanding of international issues, experience and perspective is a very positive addition. But today's reality is that only a small percentage of experienced executives have that background. Clients know that to make it a "must" on the specification list will weed out many people who, all other things equal, have the necessary background. However, international experience is clearly a major advantage because there isn't an industry or company that doesn't think about international competition, "internationalization" of products and the need to operate in other cultures. Anyone who can bring that perspective into the company will be highly valued.

For the generation coming up through the ranks, international experience will move upward toward the essential zone on the list. In today's market, companies understand that if they sort for it on an exclusionary basis, they severely cut down their list of potential candidates. But the cut line is different for those now under age 40. If they are to have a shot at the most senior jobs, they will be expected to have *some* international experience and perspective and an understanding of operating cross-culturally.

In many ways, this is the most important chapter in the book. The "message from the market" to would-be senior managers is clear. There are ten criteria to an executive profile that transcend industry and job function. All candidates are expected to have at least eight, preferably nine, elements of this profile, and must have *all* of the top five. If you don't develop your portfolio of these skills and experiences, you will never get past the quarterfinals. Your resume will be discarded. So fill in the blanks before you expect the phone to ring.

Chapter 3

The Semi-Finals: Getting on Search Firms' Radar

Searches Are Just One Avenue

While it is true that getting into the game won't do you any good if you don't have the right qualifications, it is *also* true that you can have all the right specifications, yet labor away in obscurity and wait for the phone call that never comes. A most important point to understand is that only a minority of executive jobs are filled by outside search firms. Even if you do "register" on the search firms' radar, there are still an enormous number of opportunities out there that you won't see unless you network in other ways as well.

The majority of opportunities for promotion go to internal candidates. Joining a good company with opportunities for growth is still a key part of any career plan. This is a topic we can only address briefly. Our goal is to use the characteristics of senior positions filled by search firms to understand the characteristics of executives who are promoted. We don't pretend to offer a complete perspective on the many other ways opportunities are to be found and developed. For example, when there is no internal candidate, companies do direct hiring within their industry, because they already know the strongest people among their competitors. In many of these cases, there is no "official" opening or "official" search. Sometimes a company knows where it is short of talent, but hasn't been prompted to do something explicit about it. But if a candidate comes to the company's attention, perhaps through a friend, a customer or a supplier, or someone else in the company who knows the candidate, it may be just the impetus the company needs to act. This kind of opportunistic hiring occurs frequently.

The executive talent search process has a high degree of chance associated with it. The bigger your networking net, the more likely the right fish will swim by at the right time. Experienced HR executives estimate the single biggest source for external hires at the general manager level is the networking contacts among the hiring company's "official families," among that is the social, civic or interest groups to which the company's senior executives belong.

The other side of advancement and mobility is to be focused and proactive. You can't just wait for the phone to ring. If it becomes clear that you should move away from your company, it is relatively easy to identify the firms and jobs that represent the logical next step. Exploring these targets requires a subtle strategy of having yourself introduced to the right people by the right intermediary. The intermediary's role is to explain that while you are not looking, you have always admired company XYZ and if there were a mutual interest, you would certainly be amenable.

The risk is that no one can keep a secret. Your employer may learn you are looking around. You must also have confidence in the intermediary and she must know the target company well. An uninformed or incompetent intermediary might make contact with a person who would quickly figure out that it is his or her own job for which you could be a candidate.

The point is, there are a variety of ways to position yourself for mobility. The point of this book is to help you understand all those things you should be doing long in advance of any situations which cause one to look. As search consultants say, the worst time to begin networking is when you need it the most. The real players are doing it all the time, *especially* when things are going well.

The Top Five Factors: Nothing Beats Having a Reputation for Getting Results

Table 3.1 shows the top five factors that were relevant in putting a candidate on our search partners' radar. Not surprisingly, the list looks a lot like the one derived from the "spec sheets." But now the ordering changes. The "comparable job" factor is a big part of the search process, so it jumps up into the top tier. Stressed over and over in the interviews was that the real "sorting factor," at this stage, is the reputation for getting results. Once they conduct a round-up of those in the right jobs with the right background, the ranking is done on the record of accomplishments. How to build that record of results is the subject of all the books on general management. For our purposes, the issue is, how do you demonstrate what you have done in a way that helps you stand out from any others with similar backgrounds?

The partners we talked with all said the same thing. Colleagues, coworkers, and competitors all know who the stars are. Getting known among that group is the most important factor to improving your odds of getting on the search firms' lists. *But* there are "good" lists and "bad" lists. There are "perennial" candidates or stars who keep seeing lots of opportunities. A second group network but don't have the track record. They will never be referred to positively by a colleague or competitor. A third group have respectable records, but have alienated

TABLE 3.1   Top Five Factors That Put Senior Management Candidates on Search Firm Radar

Factor	% Very High	Rank	% High or Very High
Reputation for results	84.48	1	87.93
Ability to think strategically	72.41	2	77.59
Previous comparable position	68.97	3	82.76
Reputation for organization building	65.52	4	75.86
Communication skills	62.07	5	79.31

people, developed reputations for being difficult, self-focused or some-one who doesn't "play fair." Remember this before you make enemies or burn bridges. Make sure the stakes are high enough to risk making an adversary who would like nothing better than to seek revenge.

Secondly, recognize that upward mobility is "presumptive," that is, people who are promoted regularly are assumed to have achieved results. The flip side is that it's harder, even if true, to convince people that you have achieved positive results if your employer has kept you in the same job for ten years. If your moves don't demonstrate a clear pattern of tak-ing on broader responsibilities, you need to think about whether you should do something about it. Both lateral moves and long periods with-out new assignments or advancements are viewed suspiciously.

Third, a reputation for results is carried farther if you are visible in your own industry. Visibility comes from writing, presentations and speeches, and from reciprocating in benchmarking initiatives both with competitors and with customers and suppliers. Take the long view. Peo-ple who see these as a waste of time are penny-wise and pound-foolish.

Another significant way of getting a reputation for results involves understanding how much of the employer's reputation rubs off on you. Warren Buffet is reported to have said, "When a manager with a rep-utation for brilliance joins an industry with a reputation for being dif-ficult, it is the reputation of the industry that will survive." That is equally true for "star" companies, i.e., those that are perceived as hav-ing superior reputations, doing exciting things, or have been the train-ing grounds for future winners. Search consultants refer to certain organizations as "academy companies," training ground of the industry elite. That is not to say that doing a good job at a less well-known com-pany makes it impossible for someone to find you. But it means a sec-ond step must be added. There must be evidence that either you were brought in to effect a turnaround, or that something special is occur-ring because of you. There is a penalty for working in a company in trouble, or one with a reputation for being a laggard, out of touch, or behind the times. It is not insurmountable, but it is real.

Getting on the Database

All searches start with basic research by the search firm. This research typically takes three forms. You have essentially no chance of being dis-covered unless your name turns up in one of these three ways.

The search firm first develops a list of companies that will have people with the right experience, values, and reputations. It then looks to determine the incumbents of the positions that would be considered qualifying. We stress that with the increased use of sophisticated databases to do this first round search, *it is important that you have a conventional job title.* When the searches of annual reports, directories and proxies are done, they are done by job title, and your name will get sorted onto the preliminary list if you have a "standard" job title. Firms that use less descriptive, less hierarchical titles (affiliate, partner, facilitator, etc.) may help people feel good but may be hurting their mobility. So it is not a trivial issue that you have a conventional job title that reflects the scope and traditional description of your kind of position.

This is no minor challenge with companies flattening hierarchies and becoming more "warm and fuzzy." It is not inconceivable, as the vice president of manufacturing, to be offered the redesignation as "partner for physical processes" or "the colleague for product assembly." There is a price to be paid, and it is that the computer search of comparable positions kicks your name out into the "reject" bucket because it can't figure out what your nontraditional title means.

In addition to being at the right company with the right title, you also want to be where the action is, because the second phase of research is to look at companies where change is occurring, where people are exposed to cutting-edge issues. When companies go through new product cycles, mergers, or downsizing, other firms feel they can learn from the pioneers. Also, where there is some disruption going on, the search firm feels people might be a little bit more willing to listen to an outside offer.

The third phase of research is targeting companies that are the most successful competitors, whose values and practices the recruiters admire or who they feel have surmounted challenges analogous to those the successful candidate will face in his or her new position.

Jumping onto the database is, in large measure, an ongoing process of continuing to focus on several questions. "Are you in the middle of the action?" "Are you and your company at the front end of forward thinking and change?" and "Does your personal profile reflect positively on your own reputation within the company?" There are two other common sense suggestions. One is to make sure you are listed in annual reports, organizational charts, customer service brochures, etc. If your company doesn't do annual reports or doesn't do organization listings at your level, you might think about publishing those kind of things for your customers and suppliers with an understanding that they will also get into the hands of search firms to keep their databases up to date. Another way of having your name show up in the databases is to write articles for magazines, be a seminar speaker and serve in the trade and industry organizations as an officer, director or a resource. Search firms learn of you through these conduits.

Networking: The Most Important Thing of All

Network . . . network . . . network . . . all the time and especially when you don't need it and when things are going well.

Search consultants understand that organizational charts, company phone books, listings in annual reports and job descriptions are static, meaning they don't indicate what is really going on within the company. The best source of information is people in and around the industry. Search firms rely on these people to provide opinion, perspective, judgments on quality and reputation. Only people can provide the history and background that allows a search firm to assess if someone is the right kind of candidate or just happens to be occupying a "qualifying" place, but has none of the other desired traits.

SEARCH FIRM SECRETS

What Networking Means in Practice

- ✓ Serve with your industry or trade associations.
- ✓ Participate in benchmarking studies.
- ✓ Write thought pieces.
- ✓ Be active in service and civic groups.
- ✓ Talk to other people about their work; learn who does what.
- ✓ Be helpful.

WORKING THE OBVIOUS NETWORKS

Whatever else, make sure you are not an invisible member of the organization. You must become a name with a reputation. Also, become visible among customers and suppliers. There is networking and then there is *effective* networking. It does no good to be on the masthead of organizations, but invisible in practice. It makes no sense to join a club or trade group and never attend the meetings. It makes no sense to be a passive, or negative, member since your reputation will be for how you behave *within* the trade or industry group. It will be assumed that is the same style you bring to your job. When involved in these organizations, be just as professional, enthusiastic, helpful, creative and dynamic as you are on the job. Take the leadership roles, be self-effacing, but willing to work. Build your reputation within the groups as a doer or leader, thoughtful, respectful and yet interesting. That will be the reputation attached to you when people ask about you from the outside.

THE NOT-SO-OBVIOUS NETWORKS

Earlier in this chapter we discussed how many job searches are never really "officially" opened, but exist only if someone makes a suggestion to someone who has been thinking about an opening or a need to solve a problem. What becomes more important is the less obvious networking that people should do, especially as they become more senior. Senior searches will go beyond the industry to look for people with broad general management skills. That is why, as executives mature, they become involved in school alumni organizations, civic groups, political organizations, charitable groups, common interest groups. They find it has a triple payoff. It entails the intrinsic value of giving back, rewarding in its own right. The second payoff is the opportunity to meet people outside an industry group, to develop a broader range of acquaintanceships. (A life where most of your primary relationships are among coworkers or industry colleagues will be narrow and dull.) The third payoff is another network of people who may think of you when opportunities arise outside your industry.

Handling the First Phone Call

UNDERSTAND THE PROCESS AND THE STAGES

When that first phone call comes in from a search firm you don't know, the search consultant may not know whether you are a potential candidate or someone who could give them leads. The first rule is, *don't answer too quickly*. Our partners say listen, listen quietly and listen carefully. Even if it is something in which you have no interest, understand you are being evaluated not only as a candidate but as a person who might be a future candidate. If you turn off someone at this stage, you are going to cut yourself off for future opportunities to build a reputation within the search firm community. If a consultant phones, say, "Great, how can I help you." You don't have to declare yourself interested or not interested. Just take the call, don't be aloof and offer help if you can.

PLAYING HARD TO GET WILL MAKE YOU HARD TO GET (AND HARD TO FIND)

A second piece of advice is to understand that at these early stages, there is no negotiating going on. Faking disinterest, because you feel that is a better posture than seeming too eager is unproductive. You don't want to get ahead of either yourself or the natural stages of the searches. You don't need to declare yourself right away. If it does become clear that you are being approached as a potential target, say you're flattered, hadn't really thought about this, but will have to think about it, and would like more information. As long as you are, in good faith, doing due diligence, everyone respects that. The key is, of course, if you get to the point where you have concluded that you have no interest, then communicate that quickly before any more time is invested in you by the search firm or the client.

DESCRIBE THE RESULTS YOU HAVE ACHIEVED SUCCINCTLY, CLEARLY AND CANDIDLY

If you are someone who they might be interested in, they'll ask for a description of what you have done. Here, remember again, you are being evaluated not only on what you have accomplished, but on how you handle a situation like this. A long discussion of jobs, titles, responsibilities and processes you have handled will be counterproductive. People are looking to understand what your specific contribution was to tangible results, so describe the key outcomes for which you were unambiguously responsible. Quickly focus on the bottom line, e.g., "I was the general manager of the dry cereal group for two years. My two biggest accomplishments were the introduction of the new brand Captain Smackey's that built $5 million in volume and achieved profitability in less than two years, and increasing the overall growth rate on dry cereals from the 6 percent it had been in the past ten years to 7.5 percent in the last two." If asked, tell how you did it, but don't get into all the cute tricks and promotions. Show that you think and focus on the bottom line and that you expect the search consultant to ask the detailed questions where and when interested.

NEVER EXAGGERATE, NEVER OBFUSCATE, NEVER ELIMINATE IMPORTANT TIMES, PLACES OR EVENTS

I asked all of our partners what the worst thing is that clients or candidates can do in the early rounds. They all said the same things: exaggerating their role or their connection to certain results; embellishing on their job titles or education; obfuscating why they made certain moves or what prompted certain changes, whether something was a promotion or a lateral move, or omitting certain jobs or positions or blank periods in their resume. Those can never be withdrawn or changed. No matter how good you are or even how good the reasons might be, if there is an inconsistency between what you say in that first interview and what comes out later, you are certainly out of the running for this job. And you have substantially reduced your potential to stay on the Rolodex. So no matter what the temptation is, be direct. Be honest about the degree of your involvement. Don't weasel around situations where you were either fired, quit or had gaps in your resume. Give other people credit for results and acknowledge that yours was one of several roles in a major success. This will lead people to assume you are being modest. They will give you more credit than if you took it yourself. If you are caught overplaying your role, even by a small degree, you have done yourself permanent harm.

UNDERSTAND THE SEARCH CONSULTANT'S OBJECTIVE DURING THE FIRST INTERVIEW

The most important advice is not to get ahead of the process. You may be one of a dozen people who the research indicates is worth getting to know. The consultant is not in a position to offer you the job, or even make you a semifinalist at this point. What he needs is enough background to answer these three questions for the client:

1. Do you meet all or most of the criteria for the job in the spec sheet?

2. In the course of the phone call did you handle yourself in a way that suggests you have the interpersonal skills, maturity,

judgment and communication skills to match the other job requirements?

3. Are there any reasons why, no matter what, you couldn't or wouldn't be able to act on this opportunity, i.e., you are under contract, you have a noncompete agreement, you are precluded from moving because of family issues or strong geographical preferences, etc.?

The point is, if you got the phone call, you're on the radar. Your goal is to stay on the radar for this and other opportunities. If you are interested, in an appropriate time and way, you will be considered for the next round. It is too early to negotiate, posture, and way too early to ask about salary, benefits or perks. The search consultant will ask your own salary history and make the judgment as to whether you are in the ballpark. Again, resist all temptation to evade or exaggerate, since the consultant can verify it anyway. All you want to do is have the phone call end with the search consultant feeling you handled yourself well and that you're the right kind of candidate for this job, or a person to keep in mind for another search.

Being a Good Source

Most people who are candidates and are thought of regularly for executive assignments have also served as good sources to the search firms. Advice on how to be a good source includes:

TAKE ALL THE CALLS

Don't have your secretary screen out calls from search firms. In many cases they may not identify themselves, in part because they are trying to protect you from people knowing you are talking to a search firm. When someone calls to "source" a job, spend a little time thinking about the job. Listen, even if you are not interested, and see if you can make a contribution. Don't ever run your own agenda in terms of the names you give them. Several partners mentioned that there is a tendency to help friends. If you are in the service business, you might mention people who you think, if they get the job, might be future customers. But that becomes obvious very quickly. Don't recommend someone who you know wouldn't be a strong candidate because you figure it will create a favor owed to you. That person won't get the job anyway and all you will do is ruin your own reputation with the search firms. Do give them other sources if you can't think of good candidates. Give them names of those who might know other sources. That is important information to them and it shows that you are connected. Don't feel like you have to do it off the top of your head. Ask them to send you a copy of the job description. Tell them you will think about it and then get back to them within a week. Even if nothing occurs to you, the consideration and the fact that you have thought about it will be impressive. It is perfectly all right to call back, and say you have thought about it and still no specifics come to mind, but you'll get back if something comes up.

Do You Want to Be a Reference?

This is a tough area because of legal and emotional risks. When someone tells you she gave your name to a search firm as a reference, it is that person's presumption that you will say nice things. If your opinion is other than totally positive, you have some real issues. Do you respond evasively, or, if you are candid, how can you prevent the person from knowing that you might have spoiled her chances? On balance I encourage you to, in fact, serve as a reference as long as you feel that you are dealing with people who can maintain the confidence, and that you can be candid. If all you are going to do is say the same about everyone or if you are going to be so vague as to be useless, then stay away. Even without being overly negative, search firm partners are good at reading people who try to point out problem areas. Don't be afraid to let them into your thinking.

Networking with the Search Firm

Once you have made it onto the database, done your networking with the industry groups, been approached once or twice for jobs, and been used as a source, the key question is how to maintain contacts with the search firms. All recruiters say it is important and useful that they keep in touch with people who might ultimately be candidates, as well as sources, but keep these important warnings in mind. The first is not to be a time waster. All search consultants are perpetually busy. They are on the phone, traveling, meeting clients, meeting candidates, developing sources. Time is their only resource. Be respectful of that reality and understand that they can get most of what they need in terms of keeping up with you and your situation in five or ten minutes at certain appropriate stages. Trying to have a ninety-minute lunch every three months with a series of search consultants will only get you labeled as a time-waster.

REMEMBER WHO THEY WORK FOR

Search consultants are engaged by clients. It is not their responsibility to help people look around for better jobs. The typical executive search consultant might have four to six searches at any one time and those must occupy the majority of her time and attention. The odds that your interests fit any of that small number of searches at a particular time is very low. Your first goal is to have the search consultant keep your file in the database up to date. Your second goal is to be the kind of person about whom the search partner will have positive things to say when a database search hits your name.

REMEMBER THAT SEARCH FIRMS MUST KEEP THEIR DATA FRESH

The half-life of what is in the search firm's files is only six or seven months. Search firms know that whatever they have on file about you that is more than four or five months old must be verified before they can do anything with it. Say to yourself, "Has something happened to my circumstances that would cause my files to need updating? Is my file accurate and complete?" In many cases, there is nothing that you would pass on that would be new news to them. So you might want to be circumspect about making a contact. On the other hand, when you have had a promotion, a transfer, or if you have just achieved something significant, it is time to call. Also, if you know that within the next year or so you are likely to be asked to do something different in your current company, you should consider that to be a good time to catch up with your contacts in the search business. A brief phone call or little note that says, "Here is something that I hope you will add to my file; call me if you want to chat," is all it takes. If the news is a prospective promotion or reassignment, it is also understandable that you would want to get an outside opinion on whether it is a desirable change.

WHEN NOT TO CALL

The worst time to make a call is when you are angry or frustrated with your company. The worst time to call is when you are feeling like you have to find a new set of alternatives. Your attitude will show thorough. Every search consultant knows exactly when someone is calling because he or she is fed up with the current employer. You must let the moment pass. That is not to say that you should ignore those feelings, but let the irritation of the moment subside. Look at the broader sweep of events. If there hasn't been a promotion or accomplishment recently, structure the contact in the context of a three-to-four year perspective on what you have done and what your goals are for the next two or three years. Anything that suggests urgency of action or a frustration or disappointment is not going to help the cause, nor is the search consultant typically in a position to do anything within the short term.

How to Handle Rejection

Even the most successful and skillful executives will be told they are not among the semifinalists or finalists. The fact that, for many reasons, you were not moved to the next round is more a reflection on the peculiarities of the search process and the specifics than it is any reflection of you. Search firms are not in the habit of talking to losers or failures, and you should never feel any sense of disappointment. Nor should you argue with the search firm about its conclusions. In many cases the client may have something specific that he wanted in terms of background that you don't possess. It is optional for you to ask for feedback. There can be things that you can learn, although the reasons why you might not have fit one specific opportunity are not necessarily things that you want to let shape you for future searches. You might want to learn whether it was your profile, or the nature of your skills, that washed you out. Probably the most important thing you would want to learn is whether there were issues of style or reputation, or how you handled the process, that knocked you out of the box. Like bad credit reports, those kinds of things can become part of the "book" on you that would be hard to deal with if you didn't know about them.

The reality is that people don't like to say negative things directly. You are not likely to get candid feedback if you ask, "What did I do wrong, where did I mess up, where didn't I stack up well?" The general response will be there was nothing wrong with you, it was just the client was looking for something a little different. Ask in slightly different form. Ask what the candidates who moved to the next round had in common. Questioned in that form, search consultants will, at least obliquely, point out the items that the other candidates possessed that you didn't. If you don't hear much about differences in experience or position, it does at least raise the question of whether skill differences or style got in the way.

Keep in mind that people are very reluctant to give negative feedback, so you have to make an opening statement that invites personal feedback. An open-ended, "Gee, did I do anything wrong?" is not likely to get you anything other than an evasion. On the other hand, you might say, "Well, as I listen to you I don't see too many differences in background, but I had a funny feeling that I was not connecting with you." Or, you might say, "I felt like perhaps I didn't do a good job of describing the things that I have accomplished." Those phrases will give the search consultant an opportunity, if that is, in fact, part of the issue, to give you hints or suggestions.

SEARCH FIRM SECRETS

How to Handle Coming in Second
- ✓ It happens to everyone.
- ✓ It's still a compliment.
- ✓ Don't challenge the conclusion.
- ✓ Use it as an opportunity for feedback.
- ✓ Remember, better fit doesn't mean more capable.

The point is that you want to be considered for many opportunities. You want to be candid about the opportunities where you are not interested and be realistic that many of the ones that come won't be right. In some cases, you won't fit, or someone else will have a better profile. Your goal is not to be offered *every* job, but to be considered for those where there is possible mutual interest. Build your reputation as someone who is worth talking to over the long term. Then, when the right one does come around, it will be a pitch that will be served up and you will be given a chance to swing at it.

Chapter 4

The Finals: How Clients Pick the Winning Candidate

Understand the Process

Often, candidates hurt their chances or become frustrated by trying to move the search process along faster than it typically goes. Or, more significantly, they attempt to skip one of the basic steps, or take them out of sequence. The most common mistake is to begin the negotiation too early. They start playing coy or focusing on changing the parameters of the job as presented. Partners say that candidates often don't understand that, early in the process, they are just one of many alternatives. For a candidate who is ultimately selected as the target there will be opportunities later to negotiate and/or reshape the parameters of the job. But to attempt to do so while the candidate is just one of the many who may or may not be an attractive fit removes him from consideration or places a cloud over his candidacy.

Almost all searches follow a very similar pattern. In the second stage—getting on the radar screen—the consultant may contact ten or fifteen candidates based on research or referrals. They may conduct interviews with five to ten of those candidates, based on the criteria referred to in the previous chapter. At this stage the partner may conclude that some are not appropriate for the position. That can be because the fit to the specifications isn't good, or the skills required aren't in evidence, or a candidate "bombs" the interview. (See Chapter 6, "Sixteen Ways to Blow a Job Interview".)

For those candidates that the search consultant feels have a reasonable chance of becoming finalists, a presentation report is prepared, and reviewed with the client. It is a lengthy narrative that outlines the candidate's employment history in great detail, describing the candidate's specific contributions, achievements and the practical role he or she had in various jobs. It discusses the reasons behind changes in positions or moves from one company to another. And it deals with impressions, communication style, thinking, appearance, mannerisms, energy level and enthusiasm. It discusses background factors relative to potential interest: does the person feel this is the kind of job that might be attractive; is it a good or bad time to consider a move; are there personal factors that would influence an ultimate decision, e.g., geographic or family priorities, etc.? The report also discusses compensation history.

It is important for candidates to understand that, while they might have had several discussions with a researcher from the search firm, a phone conversation or even two with a search firm partner, and an extensive interview, they are still just one of a relatively long list of names about whom the client may not even have a great deal of information. To presume that one is being offered the job at this stage is a mistake. But neither should candidates feel that they are being asked to make binding decisions. At the end of the process, if there is some reasonable chance of interest, the conversations can be continued. No one expects a final response until a specific offer, with details, is pending. But similarly, you improve your reputation with the search firm community if, while being helpful in terms of providing other ideas, you are clear if and when you reach the point where there is no chance that you would consider this proposal if it were offered.

The next step may vary depending on the client and the nature of its relationship with the search firm. Some clients want to see all presentation reports and a specific recommendation for each candidate. The recommendation will tell the client whether this is someone the employer should definitely see, is someone who isn't going to end up as one of the two or three leading candidates, or someone who should be put on hold until the shape of the competing field becomes clear. In other cases the presentation reports are used as a briefing on those candidates advancing to the next step in the process, which is visiting with the client firm.

Typically search firms present two or three candidates for interviews with the company. From a candidate's point of view, even after having spent a day or two, or even more, visiting with the hiring manager and/or board of directors committee, there should be a clear awareness that there are at least one or two others going through the same process. Being sensitive to perceptions of what the client views as appropriate at each stage is critical to becoming the *top* candidate.

STAGE ONE—LET'S LOOK FOR OURSELVES

The best candidates understand that most searches go through four stages. There is little to be gained, and much to be lost, in accelerating or rearranging these stages. In the first stage, the candidate is essentially an unknown even though the client might have read the presentation report, or have some background from the search firm or even from other sources. Firms know they must do their own due diligence. They want to answer for themselves the question, "Does this candidate have what it takes to succeed and contribute productively and harmoniously in *our* environment?" So while they are certainly willing to accept the search consultant's recommendation, until they see for themselves, the candidate is still an unknown.

The first order of business is to question whether the candidate meets the primary specifications of the position. Answering this question almost always means focusing on relevant experiences in industries or situations that are comparable or transferable, and finding a record of demonstrated achievement. Comparable position and reputation for results are the items that must be addressed first.

The reality is that search firms are good at what they do. Very few candidates fall out at this stage on those factors. This initial stage often serves just to reinforce the conclusions of the search firm that the basic specs have been met.

STAGE TWO—DO WE LIKE YOU?

Stage two is what several partners characterized as the "do we like you, would we like working with you" phase, dealing with the broad issues of cultural fit. By the time someone has become a finalist, most of the sorting is done on cultural fit. The other factors have long been satisfied in the screening process, so this is where the game is won or lost. The dimensions are quite different from case to case. In some, fit is strictly the issue of "personal chemistry" between the firm and the candidate. But more often it is the much more complicated issue of fit with the company's "culture," is she "one of us"?

STAGE THREE—DO YOU LIKE US?

The third phase turns to the question of, "Are you excited about us, would you feel proud and motivated to work here, is this something that we both see is in your long-term interest to do?" This is just a variant of the wanting-to-be-liked issue. No company management wants to hire someone they believe will look down on them or the company. Hiring executives do not want to hire someone who will feel that he is too good for the situation or is looking past it as a stepping-stone until something better comes along. It is also the important stage of wanting to avoid rejection. If you have three candidates, all of whom are similarly qualified, your preference would be to make your first offer to someone who is likely to accept. Hiring executives do not want to report to the board of directors that the top candidate turned them down. There is also the important ingredient of confidence, enthusiasm and optimism. People understand that executive jobs are challenging, risky and uncertain. Enthusiasm, optimism and positive thinking are often critical factors. Some candidates come across as overly concerned about whether the job can be done successfully, or whether the company will support them, or whether it is the right thing for them to do. There is a tendency to assume that that same attitude will translate into a tentative approach to the job itself. This may not be true, but the "reluctant" candidate may never get a chance to prove it.

STAGE FOUR—THE OBJECT OF OUR AFFECTION

During these first three phases, if a candidate raises too many concerns or issues, even those that are appropriate, he can easily derail his candidacy. But the good news is that there is a time and place for raising them. The candidate who understands the process knows that issues can be raised at a time when the candidate has more leverage. That leads us to the fourth phase. The pecking order of candidates is now established. Individuals who, in the first three stages, are viewed as applicants, now become objects of affection and will be pursued aggressively. Understanding the psychology is important. Having invested all of the time and effort in the process and having committed themselves, the candidate is now endowed with the imprimatur of the client's own judgment. The client develops a sense that the world is now looking at them and deciding whether they are going to be attractive enough to land this candidate. In phase four, the tables turn. This is the point where discussions about compensation, benefits, issues of authority, resources, job dimensions and future career paths can be raised without jeopardizing the candidacy. A little later on we talk about some of the negotiating do's and don'ts. We'll discuss the trade-offs between having direct conversations and using agents or attorneys. But the key point is that all good candidates understand the grand sweep of the process. They realize that it can be dealt with only on its own terms. They realize that using the momentum of the process at the right time is as much an important skill as meeting the spec sheets and all the other explicit factors that go into an executive search.

Winnowing Down to the Finalists

Table 4.1 shows how the five factors rated most important in the final stage of a senior level executive search don't, in fact, change very much

TABLE 4.1 What Makes Acceptable Final Candidates—Factors Ranked 1–5

Factor	% Very High	Rank	% High or Very High
Reputation for results	81.03	1	93.10
Interpersonal skills	79.31	2*	89.66
Communication skills	79.31	2*	91.38
Ability to think strategically	74.14	3	86.21
Previous comparable position	68.97	4	87.93
Fit with company culture	67.24	5	77.59

*Tied for second place.

from the client specs. The most important factor is still a reputation for results. At this level and at this stage of the process, no one is going to take a chance on somebody who hasn't proved her capabilities in a comparable situation. The other top factors are again interpersonal and communication skills, and the ability to think strategically. Fit with the company culture rounds out the top five. The relative ranking really hasn't changed much. But in practice, the sorting has moved the important discriminating threshold away from reputation, through skills, toward cultural fit.

I asked why many search consultants stressed interpersonal and communication skills in the second stage and cultural fit in the third, yet the responses to the survey really showed them staying relatively constant. The answer was the logical one. In going through the three stages, they said, we are sorting *in* and sorting *out*. The first thing they sort for, in the research, is the comparable position and reputation for results. That is what gives them their targets. Then, in the interviews with the candidates, they are really trying to pick up on the communication and interpersonal skills. In stage two they sort *out* any people who really don't bring those skills to the table. So by the time they get to the visits with the client, if they have done the job right, all the finalists ought to be above the specs in terms of these first four characteristics. The principal issues left are cultural fit and chemistry.

Tables 4.2 and 4.3 show the clustering of factors in this finalist stage for the middle five and bottom five factors. The relative rankings don't really change very much. Some of the things that are somewhat more

TABLE 4.2 What Makes Acceptable Final Candidates—Factors Ranked 6–10

Factor	% Very High	Rank	% High or Very High
Reputation for organizational building	62.07%	6	77.59%
Sales and marketing experience	58.62%	7	77.59%
Previous P&L (line management)	56.90%	8	74.14%
Previous industry experience	55.17%	9	81.03%
Charm and charisma	43.10%	10	67.24%

TABLE 4.3   What Makes Acceptable Final Candidates—Factors Ranked 11-15

Factor	% Very High	Rank	% High or Very High
Background in specific technology	37.93%	11	51.72%
Advanced degree	34.48%	12	51.72%
Reputation with industry group	27.59%	13	44.83%
Physical appearance	24.14%	14	55.17%
International experience	18.97%	15	48.28%

important in terms of putting people on the radar at the middle stage (like having an advanced degree, attending a prestigious school or having been active civically or politically) have diminished in consequence. Most candidates in this final stage have either satisfied these criteria or there is something specific about the candidate's background experience that overrides the "nice but not necessary" elements.

Assessing Communication and Interpersonal Skills in the Finals

In Chapter 3 we talked about why these skills are so important. We also talked about how search consultants determine whether a particular candidate has the ability to think strategically. It is important to remember that, in this process (like a beauty contest), scores from preliminary rounds don't carry forward. You may have made the finals because the search consultant was impressed with your interview, but all you did was make the finals. You are starting over dead even relative to the other candidates. It is the score that you get from the client relative to those other candidates that matters almost exclusively. This is obviously a factor that candidates must understand. In the candidate's mind, she has told her story two or three times already. The candidate may feel that everybody has already heard it, and may therefore either truncate it or speak with less enthusiasm and energy. The result can easily be that the client goes back to the search consultant and says, "Boy I didn't see that energy and confidence you talked about in your report." The difference, of course, was that the candidate did not understand that the interview with the search firm was a rehearsal. It is only what the critics say on opening night that matters.

The other area where communication and interpersonal skills are tested and assessed is in the multiple interviews with company officials. Again, there is always the risk that the candidate will run out of energy or let down. This may be especially true with some of the people that he may think are less important. Candidates may believe that if they impressed the "big" boss, or the board of directors, that is enough. In reality, if it is deemed important enough for someone to visit with the candidate, that person's perception is included in the final decision. While those who interview the candidate may vary in importance within the company, even one negative vote or reservation can be the deciding factor when candidates of comparable background and skill are in the running. Search partners say this is one of the harder things to do where there are multiple interviews and multiple rounds involved. Candidates must find the right fine line between being confident but not condescending; being proud of achievements but not caught up in self-promotion. You must display that you are a good listener and that you are empathic. And you must recognize that in a relative short period it is your responsibility to do the sales job and not hope that the interviewer will somehow coax the data out of you by asking the right questions.

The assessment of strategic thinking skills is another key part of the process of selecting finalists. A candidate's strategic thinking skills are often judged by the nature of the questions the candidate asks. This operates in parallel to the notion of understanding which kinds of questions fit which phase. When you are still in the applicant phase, the questions you should be asking are about the company's strategy, opponents, opportunities, current strategic thinking and changes in the industry. These kinds of questions make it clear that you know how to collect data and assemble a strategic vision; that you can assess whether the company is in a place that makes sense; and that you know how to cope with shifting times and circumstances. It also is a good way to avoid getting into the "what's in it for me" questions. Those must be deferred until you have become the target of company interest. Without ever saying so, you must effectively communicate your confidence in the company—that it will know how to provide any manager with the right kind of authority, support, resources and compensation. Your attitude that these things do not need to be explored early or in depth is a compliment that must be paid.

Similarly, the way in which you describe your history is another important way that clients assess the strategic level on which you operate. Open-ended questions like, "What is the hardest thing you ever did?" "What is the thing that you felt most proud of?" "When you took this job, what did you think you could achieve?" are all trying to get at the same thing. As one of the partners said, "If someone can't describe his contribution concisely, in under five minutes, by starting with an overview of the situation, the strategic options, the ones he chose and why he chose them and how he moved the organization to implement that strategy, then the candidate has failed both my 'ability to communicate' and 'strategic thinking' tests." Partners have said the same thing by referring to the negative reaction they have to people who at 15 minutes are still reciting a sort of undifferentiated chronology of, "And then I . . . and then I . . . and then . . . " This shows no ability to operate with strategic perspective. Even worse is the person who describes himself or herself as a passenger on a train of circumstances. When the connection between a candidate's vision and the company's results is unclear even in the candidate's mind, it can hardly inspire a sense of leadership.

Cultural Fit: "The Final Frontier"

WHY FIT IS SO IMPORTANT

We hinted at it early in the chapter. Everyone we talked to stressed how fit is, in fact, the principal task that both the search consultant and the hiring manager are ultimately paid to assess. It is important because, without it, the odds of the new executive's successfully achieving the goals that the company established for the position are critically compromised. But *why* is that so? Why is this "fit" thing so important to results? In some cases it is strictly the self-esteem factor. People want to be liked. If they are admired and they admire someone like themselves, it reinforces their own sense of self-worth. So at the simplest level, fit is just one of those things that makes the interactions among the leadership of a company run more smoothly.

In all cases we studied, the position was for a senior executive. The issue of fit went beyond minimizing friction and maintaining a positive relationship among the parties. Fit is often a key part of the reason that the senior position is open in the first place. So, in addition to looking for an executive who can fit within an existing structure or style, the challenge is often more complicated. This element of fit means a fit with what the company is likely to become, or needs to become. Fit changes where the environment is changing, where the competitors are changing, where one generation may be retiring and a new generation moving up. There is often a clear understanding that the new leadership must be more in tune with a changing set of environmental demands and a new set of dynamics within the company. Often the target for the recruiting firm is to find someone who comes from a culture that has been through the kind of changes that are anticipated at the company.

This brings up the third type of fit. This is to find someone whose culture is what the company aspires to become. In these cases the client not only understands that change is occurring, but has decided that a certain style and approach will be needed to achieve success. An outside executive is being recruited because he likely brings the kind of cultural experiences and style that can reshape the company. Search firms will be told, "Bring me a new president who can make our culture like that of Pepsi." This is code for wanting aggressive, targeted, competitive, risk-taking, innovative executives. Or they will say, "I want somebody to make us the Motorola of our industry." This is shorthand for globally oriented, focused on product quality, product innovation and a sophisticated people-oriented leadership mixed with a fact-based, decision-making mind-set.

"I Don't Know How to Define Fit but I Know It When I See It"

This is what many executives and search consultants say when asked how they judge a right fit. One partner put it this way: "The most important dimensions to senior management are being a strategic thinker, a visionary and having people and team-building skills. But most finalists have those. The essence of what we do is chemistry. We find people who meet the specifications and we confirm that everything they say about their background is true. That's the stuff that's a mile wide and an inch deep. The art is trying to predict the chemistry between the candidate and the firm." As I pressed, some of the better answers are the simple ones. When I ask how partners tell if there will be a cultural fit, a number of people explained that it all starts with people who are relaxed with the search process. They understand fit; they know that every job isn't for them; they are not trying to be things that they are not. These people will pull away from circumstances that will be culturally uncomfortable to them regardless of what attractions there might be.

Many partners say that the most important thing is to encourage candidates to be themselves. They help candidates understand that a bad fit hurts everyone. But the reality is people want to fill jobs. Clients will tend to overlook cultural fit because the pressure of an unfilled opening is often severe. The fact a search firm is involved usually means that something has happened so that a normal internal progression is not available. An outside candidate may be unhappy where he is and may thus be inclined to take the first interesting offer without regard to fit.

The question of how you assess what the required culture is starts with the board or the CEO (if this is not a CEO position). Search firms try to determine the existing culture, especially that of the person to whom this position reports. Also important is where the firm wants to go. Does company management believe they need someone who can fit in, or do they need someone to be an agent of change?

SEARCH FIRM SECRETS

Checklist for Cultural Fit

✓ How high is the normal energy level?

✓ Is risk-taking "good" or "bad"?

✓ How many facts do you need before you act?

✓ Do you have to look the part?

✓ Do values and lifestyle count in the work equation?

✓ Is checking with others expected or a sign of weakness?

What are the key dimensions of culture that search consultants and clients use in profiling a candidate? One partner said there were four key dimensions that he tries to understand when characterizing a company's culture. The first was energy level: is it medium, high or very high? This set a key expectation for a leadership style. Someone accustomed to a very hard-charging environment would create conflict in a company working at a more measured pace.

The second dimension is how much risk the organization will absorb. Within Pepsi, for example, which is a company viewed as aggressive and risk-oriented, the model is: "Get 80 percent of the facts and then act." People who need all the data before they can move will be uncomfortable. Conversely, a Pepsi manager in a company that wants to have every nuance buttoned up will be very frustrated. Similarly, as banks were given authority to enter the securities business they recruited investment bankers, only to quickly see them quit in frustration. The "ready, fire, aim" mentality of Wall Street collided brutally with a banking ethic that believes that 98 percent certain wasn't safe enough.

The third dimension is looking the part. In some companies a key ingredient is style, appearance and manner. No matter how talented or energetic, someone who doesn't fit the company profile will have a hard time getting along. Companies operate along a variety of points on this spectrum. In many investment banking firms, management consulting companies and some major consumer product companies like Kraft, managers say there is a certain look and style expected. Often that means having attended a "better" school, being athletic, social, expensively dressed and "well put together." Within the commercial banks there is a wider range of tolerance, but the entire range requires conservative dress and relatively high levels of decorum in style and approach.

Even firms that appear to have more tolerance for variations in dress, lifestyle and mannerisms have expectations that quickly become clear. At advertising agencies, for example, which value their nonconformity and creativity, casual dress and even wilder personal styles are all accepted. Strangely (except for the customer relations officers, known as "the suits"), the high tolerance of individual style would in fact reject someone who felt most comfortable dressing like an investment banker.

The fourth dimension of culture is the degree to which personal and family values are included in management's expectations. In some firms the spouse is expected to be an integral part of the management team. His or her willingness to participate and to be a capable "unofficial officer" of the firm can be a substantial issue. Similarly, there can be different degrees to which personal values are part of the corporate culture. It can be anything from attitude toward alcohol, tobacco, or physical fitness, to whether the political orientation of the firm is liberal or conservative. Or there's an assumed spiritual or religious orientation. In some entertainment industry firms, a free-market Republican with an assertive religious orientation would be decidedly uncomfortable. But no more so than a liberal, cause-oriented agnostic would be in one of the big service firms that grew out of a family company with fundamentalist values.

CULTURE HAS TWO DIMENSIONS: STYLE AND DECISION-MAKING

There are several other considerations that need to be explained in assessing cultural fit. One is the level of a person's aggressiveness and directness in discussion and conversation. In some firms there is an understanding that the focus is on the facts, and disagreements are expressed with brutal candor. In such firms, attacking a different point of view is perfectly acceptable. Within Motorola, for example, it is understood that indirectness or obliqueness to spare peoples' feelings is not tolerated. At the other end of the spectrum is a company like Hewlett-Packard, where a style has evolved that is very polite and sensitive. The Hewlett-Packard executive notices nuances that to an outsider might sound like perfect harmony. The insider understands a direct challenge has been raised, but all in a very different style.

A second dimension is to understand how far down the chain of command real decision-making authority exists. Organization charts and reporting relationships do not clarify this key dimension. To understand culture one must understand how decisions are *really* made. This is a different dimension than how *fast* they get made, or how much risk is acceptable, or how much information is needed. This deals with how much red tape the executive faces. It concerns how much prior notification of superiors or peers is expected before someone pulls the trigger. Most organizations have official dollar and dimension limits in terms of hiring/firing and commitment of resources. The key is to determine if, in fact, those are the real limits. In some cases they can be pro forma, and while there is a process for sign-off, it is neither material nor distracting, and the real limits are much higher. In other cases there can be stated limits but, even below them, there are expectations for prior consultation that cannot be violated without consequences.

Are decisions made by individuals or through consensus? Some companies have a clear understanding that the chains of command are focused on individual positions. In those companies, decision-making is expected from those individuals. Seeking group support, broader consensus or the comfort of a shared decision will be viewed as weakness or indecisiveness. Many American companies have this as their primary mode.

As a generalization, companies with a European tradition tend to view decision-making as a shared responsibility. In those companies, decision-making authority is not granted by holding a particular spot on the organization chart, but exists through committees. For example, European companies often have both a managing board and a supervising or outside board. While there are line executives responsible for certain areas, it is in fact the member of the managing board and his colleagues who share the responsibility for each particular "portfolio" area of the company. The members of the managing board are really both the company's collective chief executive and the senior executives in charge of the various functions. The line executives are, in American terms, the chief operating officers of their business units. They are expected to direct and police day-to-day activities, but follow strategic directions from the managing board.

Another dimension involves compensation practices. Here the spectrum begins with direct linkages such as commissions or highly structured profit-sharing schemes, and runs the gamut to compensation that is determined by position in the hierarchy. Again, people accustomed to having their salary tied to production, or volume, or profit, will become very frustrated if transplanted to an organization where the long-term results of the entire enterprise and their own relative status in the hierarchy are the key factors. Similarly, individuals from a tenure-oriented culture will experience commissions or direct profit-sharing schemes as destructive, divisive and detrimental to long-term focus and teamwork. Neither is right or wrong. Both are a matter of perspective and conditioning that are key to any executive's sense of comfort.

Another key to understanding culture is how the company uses data. On one side of the spectrum, some companies are more intuitive, and even emotional. Data do not drive decisions. Decisions are driven by how someone feels, and whether someone can argue logically that a particular direction is consistent with a vision, a theme or a strategy. Factors such as "our principal competitor is doing it," "our best customer wants it," or "the board wants it done" override data. Objections about whether the impression comes from an isolated case or is really a trend are dismissed as reluctance to act decisively or weakness of competitive spirit. At the other extreme are the data-driven companies. They view the intrusion of emotion, interaction or concern for what the other guy is doing as the useless and dangerous crutches of weak minds. A nothing-but-the-facts mind-set has its own risks. Human factors are viewed as suspect. At the extreme, of course, are those firms that suffer from analysis paralysis.

Cultural fit also has to do with personal styles and values. In addition to looking the part and the degree of conformity expected in values and lifestyle, it is often important to understand the dominant background or mind-set. Is it engineering or sales? Is it product-oriented, or financial and strategic? Different dominant backgrounds affect decision-making and are important to understanding the hidden biases and priorities involved in how the firm is run. They also color the expectations of success. Someone with a finance and accounting background, even if possessing all of the values and styles of their peers, will be viewed with suspicion in a firm where all the senior executives have come from sales. Similarly, firms that have an engineering mentality will tend to be suspicious of sales- and marketing-oriented executives. Often these expectations are nothing more than ingrained biases built up in the normal dynamic tension of company interactions during the executives' formative years.

The challenge is whether or not the company understands that its culture has become too dominated by one point of view and needs leadership with a different perspective. In today's environment in particular, there is a great need to inject global perspective into companies that historically have been able to compete well on a national or regional basis. Companies like Otis Elevator and Whirlpool have made this transition as they realized that most of the growth opportunities for elevator and home appliances would be outside the saturated U.S. market.

There is obviously no one right culture. Understanding the balance between the existing culture and the one that should be created is one of the most crucial factors that participants on both sides of the executive hiring desk need to evaluate. That, of course, raises the question of how, even if you understand the elements of culture, you get a handle on it.

Taking the Cultural Temperature

Remember, search firms see their most critical function as insuring a good cultural fit. Companies are often not objective about their culture, and candidates are often tempted to describe themselves based on what they think the client company wants to hear. So it is the search firm that is often the best source of objective judgment.

Our search firm partners all say there are four or five elements to getting a handle on a corporate culture (see Cultural Snowflake box on page 61). It starts with understanding the hiring manager and her style and expectations. But all also say that you need to meet with a variety of people beyond the person responsible for the engagement of a search firm. That means the search firm must spend enough time with peers in the company and listen to what each thinks the new occupant of the job needs to bring to the table. Clearly, conflicting expectations are something that both sides need to be sensitive to. It all starts with knowing enough of the senior executives of a firm over a long enough period to have an informed sense of these cultural factors. Without the opportunity to take this cultural temperature, the search firm won't be able to identify and recognize the key style and decision-making issues that make or break a placement.

In addition to having exposure to a range of individuals, it is useful to understand the career paths of the people who made it to the top, and understand what they believe were the key factors in their success. Many of our partners said that people who were uncomfortable talking about culture and fit as explicit topics were very willing to talk about success factors for themselves. Another way at getting at the same information is to ask about cases where someone has failed and why. This is especially important to understand if the search is occurring because of a termination. This perspective is an important part of understanding how success is measured and what drives advancement.

The search firm should also get outsiders' perspectives on the company. These are useful because there is a certain amount of self-delusion that contributes to a company's description of itself. Talk to people who once worked there and to both customers and suppliers.

Mapping the Cultural Snowflake

There are lots of ways to portray a company's culture and compare it to your own. You can make lists; you can pair up points of agreement and points of disagreement. The one I like is to map "snowflakes" for yourself and for the company in each of the two key components of culture: style and decision-making. Each snowflake is a collection of opposing characteristics, or "spokes." At the outer end of a spoke the characteristic is high or strong; near the center the characteristic is low or weak. To map a snowflake, mark each characteristic with a dot: out near the end if it's strong, close to the center if weak. Then connect the dots.

For example, in the culture diagrammed below, decision-making is autonomous and intuitive; diversity is valued and uniformity of values is not required for those who get results.

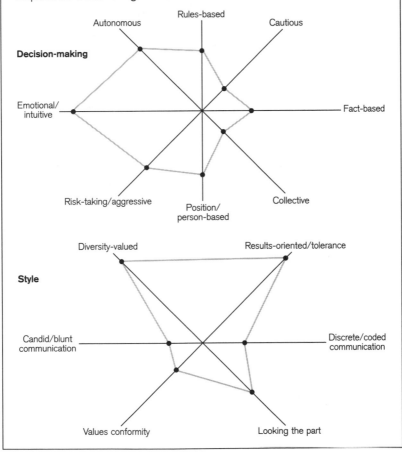

Ex-employees will tell you whether the company lives up to its mission statements for empowering employees and valuing diversity. They'll tell you whether the rank and file really understand the company's strategy and feel like they are involved in making decisions.

Suppliers will provide an honest perspective on whether quality or cost is the company's focus in relationships and/or transactions. Search consultants also know they have more homework to do when external descriptions contradict the company's self-image. While getting references on the company sounds a bit unusual, getting references on a candidate is a normal procedure. In fact, many feel referencing is most useful in the context of culture. People are not likely to provide a negative reference. In today's climate even people who tend to be candid will be cautious about describing serious problems or concerns. Giving a negative reference can now be grounds for legal action. But people are willing to talk about culture. If you ask questions like, "How effective do you believe this person is; do you think he or she is a strong leader?" or "Do you see any problems that the candidate would have in doing this kind of job; would you have any concerns?" you're going to get evasive answers. But if you say, "In terms of decision-making style, did this person make rapid decisions, or did he want to see all the facts first?" "Is this a person who is comfortable with authority, or is he inclined to want to build consensus?" you avoid the sense that any particular response will hurt someone or come back to haunt him. At this stage of the search, companies say their number one issue in working with search firms

SEARCH FIRM SECRETS

Reference Questions That Get Useful Answers

✓ Does this person protect others' feelings or feel compelled to be blunt?

✓ Does this person seek autonomy or prefer collegiality?

✓ Does this person want to fit in or stand out?

✓ Does this person always need to be right or need to be decisive?

✓ Is this person interested in good grades or learning?

is not how fast they can fill an opening, but their sensitivity to the cultural-fit issue.

The risk is that at this stage everyone is on their best behavior. Both parties need to make sure they are getting a sense of culture as it is every day, as opposed to when guests are around. For the search firm, that often means finding some kind of a "godfather" within the firm who is able and willing to escape the constraints of "corporate speak," someone who provides perspective on the real practices and priorities. The challenge is that this is hitting a moving target. It may be relatively easy to assess how good the fit is between the hiring manager and the candidate. The tougher part will be assessing how the candidate fits into the company's broader culture where it is harder to identify a single pattern. But it is understanding these unwritten rules on behavior and success paths that can make or break an executive's move from one company to another.

When Culture Clashes Become Culture Crashes

Despite all this, a substantial percentage of executive searches don't result in a good fit. People become too eager and overlook issues, or clients too eager to attract a candidate say the things a candidate may want to hear. Or candidates profess to be comfortable with a cultural pattern, but deep down inside harbor the belief that once they get inside, they can change it. The reality is that when cultural fit is ignored or faked, it's like what Woody Hays said about the passing game in football—when you throw the football there are three things that can happen, and two of them are bad. There are four things that can happen when the cultural fit is either ignored or faked by one party, and they are *all* bad.

The best case (or perhaps more accurately the least worst case) is where the candidate joins the firm and feels like a pretender, an intruder or an outsider. This cognitive dissonance can drain the enthusiasm and joy from her work and separate her from a sense of belonging and commitment. While there are many people who remain in this position, it is not a prescription for satisfaction, advancement or achievement. Both parties to a cultural misfit will unconsciously build protective barriers around themselves to reduce the irritation of this cultural clash. These barriers cut communication and reduce the ability to move with speed and confidence.

The next worst outcome is, as the result of this kind of isolation, the candidate's career stalls. The candidate not only fails to develop a sense of being on the team, but is viewed as not effective. He is not promoted and becomes at best a slot on a chart around which people maneuver. Behind this person, people feel blocked, and those above view him as part of the corporate deadwood.

The third outcome is the candidate quits in desperation, or is continually looking for other opportunities. The candidate's time with the company clearly will be seen as a resume plateau. It will raise questions about ability or judgment. Even worse, references that originate from that period will be weak and pale. This brings out one of the important rules all people considering a job change need to keep in mind. The payoff from a change that is a promotion doesn't happen *when* you make the change; it happens when you successfully *achieve* the objectives of the new position. It is a mistake to make a change when there is a high risk that the cultural fit isn't there. It's not worth the initial monetary gain or title change. If you do take a new position even though you know the fit isn't right, you misunderstand how much progress, achievement and satisfaction in the *most recent* position weigh in the evaluation of executive candidates. If you stall your career by risking a bad fit to get a promotion, you may have won one battle but lost the war.

The fourth bad thing that can happen is an explosion that results in expulsion. People become so frustrated with one another that there is a resignation or termination. Both sides feel the time together was a disaster. From company's side, nothing got done and the time was wasted. From the candidate's side, a cloud covers her career. Even if she is not fired, the jargon of the trade is that she "resigned over philosophical differences." You can be somewhat off in terms of how relevant the prior experience was. Somebody who has good basic executive skills will find that those are things that will cure themselves with time. Cultural misfits, on the other hand, not only don't cure themselves but they become more chafing with the passage of time.

Search consultants say one of the top things they want to know about candidates is what they are like when the pressure is on, when not in an interview mode. How do they behave along these cultural dimensions? The best advice I give candidates is understand what the cultural rules of the company are and be honest as to whether it is a place that will perceive you as a winner and friend, and where you will feel comfortable and happy. If you don't see that, the risk isn't worthwhile.

PART TWO

The Lessons
in Action

As a teacher, your goal is to actually achieve learning; that is, to have other people reach understanding. And the secret is not what you say but how you say it. Good teachers understand that people learn in different ways and listen in different ways. So they repeat themselves. But they don't say the same thing over and over in the same way. They make the same point and offer the same perspective but in different ways. A good teacher recognizes when that light goes on and someone reacts by saying, "When you say it that way, now I understand."

In this section we are not going to say too much that isn't inherent in the previous chapters about how executives are selected and sorted. But we will be displaying these points in a different format. We will be taking the perspective of our readers' circumstances as opposed to how the issues were identified during the study. We will also be a little more casual and use some slogans and exaggeration to make a point. Be prepared to react, at least in part, to some of this next section by saying to yourself: "But you already said that." Yes we did. If it registered with you the first time, all the better.

Why a Headhunter Makes You a Candidate

John Rau's Top Ten Reasons

There are a couple of reasons to sort all of this into a Top Ten list. Whether it is David Letterman or Moses, we have a cultural sense that ten points, ten commandments, ten anything pretty much covers the waterfront. For all senior management jobs, but especially those where one of the major search firms is involved, the scoring is like the Olympics. Unless you score in the mid to high nines you're not in the game. Your competition will have most of these factors going for them. The final selection will be between the 9.85s and 9.65s. So you have to make sure that you can score in *all* these categories.

Reason 1. *You have demonstrated the ability to get results.* Your record is of tasks completed over and above the ordinary. Your career is marked by a pursuit of challenge, responsibility and opportunity. When you describe your jobs, the end of each sentence is a result, a change. You say "We earned . . ." "We achieved . . ." "We beat . . ." Your effort is linked to something the shareholders or customers felt was better and different. You do not say, "I did," and then list activities or processes. There is evidence that you are drawn to and enjoy leadership. As early as grade school, you had jobs. You were a student leader; you mastered new skills. This pattern was constant as you grew older. It is the doing, the trying and the achieving that motivates you, not the money, or the things that come with it. You have made mistakes, recovered, and come back for more. You know mistakes don't kill you. To you, hiding from accountability is slow suffocation.

Reason 2. *You come well recommended by your peers and competitors.* Your impact and the things that you have done are obvious. Competitors know who you are and why you're effective. You have mentors among the previous generation and you are a values tutor to the generation behind you. Search firms and hiring companies live in fear of making a flawed judgment based on relatively short interactions when everyone is on their best behavior. They take great comfort from the opinion of people who are in the position to judge you over long periods.

Reason 3. *You understand who the search consultant works for and what he is trying to do.* You understand that it is not the search firm's job to get you a job or visibility. You recognize they are working for clients with specific objectives. You look to find the win–win solutions. You understand that these are long-term relationships and it is important that you play fair. You are candid and maintain credibility. You have the confidence that the only circumstances that make sense for you are those that make sense for the clients. You understand that you have the ability to say no at anytime in the process. As a result, you use the time of the search consultants and their clients wisely.

Reason 4. *You are likable, presentable and your ego is in check.* You understand that no matter how many of the other nine factors you have going for you, no search consultant is likely to take the time and the risk of presenting a candidate for whom he has to make excuses. Phrases like "You'll like him once you get to know him," "He seems a little unfriendly at first but he warms up," "He doesn't really look the part, but . . . " are not used by search firms. You are not an egomaniac, or arrogant. Search consultants and boards of directors want those who can handle all kinds of social interactions; who handle themselves in front of a crowd, and are self-effacing. They know that egotists only get worse under day-to-day pressure.

Reason 5. *You can think strategically.* You demonstrate this by the questions you ask. You know your job is to institute change in an organized direction. You know you must envision it before you can make it so. You describe your career in terms of the strategic situations you faced, decisions you made, and results you achieved. The questions you ask demonstrate that you understand strategic issues and the major levers that influence how fast and in what directions organizations can change. As discussed in Chap-ter 2, you ask about why cus-tomers pick one competitor over another. You ask about the themes that summarize competitive differences. You think "outside the box" and continually educate yourself. You look for analogs and comparisons that allow you to build strategic visions. That means you ask how the environ-ment is changing and which other industries have encountered similar changes.

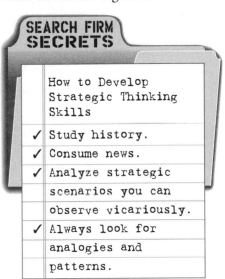

SEARCH FIRM SECRETS

How to Develop Strategic Thinking Skills
✓ Study history.
✓ Consume news.
✓ Analyze strategic scenarios you can observe vicariously.
✓ Always look for analogies and patterns.

Reason 6. *The results you have achieved have been because of the way you treat others, not in spite of it.* You don't look at the list of the ten toughest bosses and think, "Boy, someday I'll be in that group." You don't believe that fear is an effective motivator. You understand that, over time, people do their best work when they feel good about the work and good about the relationships with the people involved. You know people are more productive and creative when they are inspired, not defensive. People want to work for you because they end up feel-ing connected, stretched and encouraged to see the bigger picture. You encourage them to develop their own skills. You impart a sense of urgency, but radiate confidence that candid communication about both problems and opportunities can benefit both parties. In other words, you have a reputation for not shooting the messenger. Coworkers and subordinates don't fear hearing your voice on the other end of the phone, or face appointments with you with dread.

Reason 7. *You can sell yourself concisely.* You figure out what *they* need to know about. You don't rely on the other person's questions. You anticipate that in most steps of this process you have maybe an hour to demonstrate these ten capabilities, and you accomplish it. But you also know that a little goes a long way. In particular, you ask questions that demonstrate that your focus is on solving the company's problems. You ask what measures would indicate success, not what prerequisites go with the job. You do a lot of the selling by asking questions.

Reason 8. *You have at least some of the key specific experiences that the job entails.* You may not be in the same industry, but you have had general management responsibilities at the same level. Or you may be a level below but you bring a strong track record and understanding of the front-edge of the industry. Or you understand the key technology that is increasingly important in the new position. You are realistic about your profile as a candidate. You are not someone who thinks you could do the job, even though it is a different discipline, a different level and a different industry than the one you are in now. You understand that people are not going to take the risk that a candidate can bridge in one move more than one or two gaps between the current profile and the job's specifications.

Reason 9. *You are honest, fair, a good source, and you help search firms do their job even when there is nothing in it for you.* You take your time when somebody calls you as a source. You give them other sources and you think through the issue. You don't casually give them names that either are not high potential or where you are running some other agenda.

Reason 10. *You know who you are and what you want.* You understand the kind of environments that suit you best. You understand the kind of corporate style that makes you feel productive. You understand that it is being *successful* in a new job that is important, not just getting the job. You understand that taking a new assignment that's a bad fit is worse than not being considered at all. And you don't let either side get too far down that chain of events. You understand that if you are good, and if you follow the lessons of the search firm files, there will be many trains coming down your track.

Chapter Six

Do's and Don'ts

The Five Worst Things to Do When a Search Firm Calls

Even if you have read this book several times, when there is a message from a search firm, grab this book and read this section before you call back, and don't:

1. Be too busy to take the call. This may make you feel good. You think that by creating a sense of scarcity or high value to your time, you are enhancing your profile. But you want a long-term relationship and that starts with courtesy. The search person is always working to a deadline, and the sooner you get back, the easier it is for him to move to the next step. He may need your help to get to sources who you might identify, to reach people who you might know, or to understand your own circumstances. Someone who waits a week to call them back emits two bad impressions: either you are so disorganized that you can't prioritize, or you're so arrogant you don't care.

2. Be presumptuous that you are being offered the job. Good executives by nature are self-confident, have high self-esteem, and strong egos. Therefore when the phone rings and someone says, "I want to talk about the XYZ position," it's easy for you to assume you're the most qualified person they are ever likely to find. Unfortunately the person on the other end of the phone has a very different agenda. His thinking may be, "I have never heard of this person; I got her name from somebody else whose name I got from somebody else. All I know is that a couple of people who have some relevant perspective said you ought to talk to old Sarah X. I have about 20 minutes to figure out whether this woman is a source, a reference or even a potential candidate." They don't know whether you are going to make it easy or hard for them, or know how much time and effort to put into the conversation. So the best candidates put themselves in the search consultant's shoes and deal with it straight on. They say, "How can I help you? Tell me about the circumstances." They are honest as to whether they are a likely candidate, a source or a source of perspective. They give the consultant enough to know how to calibrate them along these dimensions. They hold the posturing until much later in the process.

3. Mislead by omission or misdirection. The first five or ten minutes of the conversation went great. It is clear that the search consultant sees you as someone who has many of the desirable profile factors and wants you to start doing a little bit of a chronology of your career. And this is when the issue of having taken off to go to Europe three weeks before the end of your MBA and flunking Statistics III and never really going back to get your degree comes up. Or the question of whether to mention that six-month period where you quit in a huff, took a disastrous job with a dinky little company, came to your senses and got back on a career track. The temptations set in. You think you can just skip over it since they may never know or care. You rationalize it wasn't that important.

The reality is you get only one chance to present the accurate record and this is it. If you are asked for highlights, you can talk highlights. But sooner or later you will be asked for a full chronology. If it is not on the first phone call, if you are in the game, it will be the second. Let the search partner decide whether an embarrassing detail is important and worth mentioning to the client. But never put him in a position where something comes up later that he didn't know. From a client's point of view, either you lied or the search consultant didn't do his job. Neither is good for your candidacy.

4. Run your own agenda. There is a great temptation when someone calls to give them the name of someone at the competition who is taking business away from you and making your life more difficult than it needs to be. Or to suggest someone within the company who is a rival, or someone who is a problem. Or someone about to be fired but who would be eternally grateful if you put his name in the game. But you must resist. These schemes always boomerang. No one is going to hire someone who is not qualified, competent or interested. It just won't get through the screens. None of your agendas will work. But what will happen is the best people will question your judgment. Or even worse, they will figure out your agenda and your credibility will be gone forever. And don't suggest names just because you think it is better to be helpful. If once you have gotten an understanding of the circumstance and nothing comes to you, don't be afraid to say so. Search partners evaluate sources by the percentage of good accurate leads that you give, not by the number of names you throw at them.

5. Forget you are being evaluated in every conversation. There is really no "off the record" when dealing with a search consultant. Never bad-mouth your employer or colleague, never tell tales out of school, never use inappropriate language or communicate disrespect for people who work for you. If you think it is macho or hip, you misunderstand the dynamic. Your goal is not to do locker room bonding with the search consultant. Make him feel confident that, in a client setting, he knows that you handle yourself appropriately.

Sixteen Ways to Blow a Job Interview

You made round one and now you are scheduled to spend the day with the clients. You made a good impression on the search partner and he has endorsed you strongly. Remember, this is like Olympic diving—your scores in the preliminary rounds don't count. You are starting from zero. It doesn't matter how big a lead you might have created over other candidates in the earlier rounds. From the client's point of view, you are all starting off the same. One bad belly flop ends the competition for you.

There are many ways to blow an interview. I list sixteen.

1. Act disinterested. Remember, there are four phases to this process and being coy during the first three is counterproductive. In the client's eyes, you are still an applicant. Even if it is true that the search consultant might have dragged you to the interview kicking and screaming, if you *act* disinterested, the client's reaction will be the same. They will wonder why you came at all. Remember you have the magic "no" card in your back pocket. You can play it anytime. But if you play it too early, you will never get a chance to understand enough about the circumstances to see if there is a basis on which a "yes" would make sense.

2. Don't do your homework. Saying, "I really haven't had time to learn much about the company, you tell me" gets you a bum's rush out the door. If you are going to come to the interview, even if your interest is light or preliminary, do homework. Show that you have invested some time in them. What you are really being judged on is how you approach important situations. If you rely on someone else to give you the facts, you are not the kind of person people want as one of their general managers.

3. Assume that the interviewer will ask all the questions you want answered. Most people aren't trained interviewers. You may be playing coy, you may just be shy or you might not want to appear too cocky, so you allow the interviewer to take the lead. When you do that, you convey the wrong attitude. Someone who handles an interview by constantly saying, "Well, what else can I tell you?" and lets the interviewer ask the questions shows a disturbing lack of curiosity and understanding. Even though you are *being* interviewed, the best approach is to ask questions about the company and the job. Show by the kind of questions you ask that you bring the right perspective. Answer open-ended questions in a way that brings out the points of your own history to demonstrate results, strategic thinking and key executive skills.

4. Forget that each interview starts from zero. You may have been through several interviews already today. It is easy to assume that somehow all of your charm and charisma gets transmitted from interviewer two to interviewer four. But don't "power down," or truncate your responses. Even worse, don't show irritation by referencing repetitive questions with "Well, when I visited with Joe, I gave him much of that background." If you see six people during an interview, and the vote is five to one because you ran out of gas or showed irritation in having to do it all over again, you may as well have blown all six.

**5. Show disregard for less senior people who may inter-
view you.** A sure way to shoot yourself in the foot. How you react if
you don't think certain people necessarily deserve to be on your schedule or deserve to be evaluating you is important. If the employer put
them there, there is a reason. You can use the opportunity with junior
people to learn about the company. Ask them about their own careers
and the things they have worked on. They will be complimented by
your interest and you will learn something about the company. They
will have felt like you have treated them like an equal. If they like you,
they can push your candidacy. Employers know that character is judged
by how you behave when you think no one important is watching.

6. Start to negotiate too early. The company will signal when
it is time to negotiate. You have to be sensitive to it. There are many
false invitations you might jump on inappropriately. For example,
someone could say, "What are the things about this job that would
attract you or that might concern you?" You might feel that is an
opportunity for questions about salary, the benefits, title or structure.
Not so. What they are interested in is your sense of enthusiasm,
whether this the kind of challenge you are looking for, and your sense
of mastery over comparable subjects. They want to know if you think
you can do the job. At some point they will make a specific offer. That's
when they'll ask you to consider this job and offer the particulars. That
is when you negotiate. You know they have to get there ultimately, so
you can afford to wait.

7. Show lack of confidence in the client. In response to
open-ended questions about concerns, don't start talking about what
happens two years out to your career. Don't question whether they will
provide the resources to help this position be successful. Both kinds
of discussions communicate a lack of confidence that they know how
to run their business. Wait until they offer the job to get these assurances where you need them.

8. Betray a confidence. You are still a guest, and still work for
someone else. You have obligations to your current employer, employees and customers. You have no obligations to the people you are interviewing, and they understand that. There is nothing awkward about
telling them you can't share things they don't need to know. Talk about
your successes and skills, not your employer's weaknesses or foibles.

Don't talk about problems that make you want to leave. Do not bring along items that are clearly the property of your current employer. That doesn't mean you are not going to get those types of questions. But no one wants to hire an executive who doesn't understand where his or her obligations are until an agreement to move to another company has been signed, sealed and delivered.

9. Show hostility toward a current or former employer. Resist any temptation for revenge, to vent or portray yourself as a victim of evil people. *You get no sympathy for portraying yourself as a victim.* You do get people questioning your judgment for getting into those circumstances in the first place. It is not because they don't understand those things can happen to everyone. The key is how you responded. If you focus on what you were leaving as opposed to what you were going toward, it is easy to conclude that you are a person who works on regrets and "could have been's." When you left employers, stress that it was to do bigger, better and more challenging jobs. Do not stress the problems or persecutions you left behind.

10. Do anything to suggest that the interview isn't the most important thing you are doing at that moment. In your mind, this may be an exploratory visit. But in the client's eyes, you are someone who is applying for the job. They need to be convinced of your interest and suitability. Don't point out that you need to cut the visit short to do something else. Don't take or make phone calls. Don't make it hard to schedule follow-up meetings.

11. Forget that they have heard everything that you have told the search consultant. So introduce new data or new perspectives very carefully. If the search consultant is likely to describe you as quite interested and positive, don't switch to indifference for the interview. If most of your focus during the conversation with the search consultant was about your experience in the most recent job, don't assume that whole subject has been covered and you can spend all your time talking about other parts of your career. Remember, you are there because the search consultant recommended you. The client is trying to confirm that that is the right judgment. Any big differences between what the search consultant said and what goes on during the next interview raises questions.

12. Take credit for things you didn't do. This comes up repeatedly. Never imply any degree of involvement that really wasn't there, or claim a link to results that may not be totally yours. As the process moves ahead, many people will be asked about you. They'll be asked specifically about your role in key results. Since one of the hardest things to do is establish the linkage between your actions and certain achievements, those are the ones tested on the outside. People make their own judgments about your likability, communication skills, your ability to think strategically. But when they go outside for references, it is to prove that what you said about what you did is straight up. Let them always be positively surprised.

13. Hide holes in your resume. Everyone can smell a situation that didn't work out, a downsizing or period of plateau. Today there is no shame in being the victim of a merger. If in fact you were fired, be direct and nondefensive if you are asked. If you made a bad decision and bailed out after six months, or a year, deal with it and move on. Someone attempting to hide things is not the kind of person I trust with major parts of my organization.

14. Pretend to be something that you are not. In the best of interviews people display good self-awareness. They understand who they are and what they are like. They know where they fit on the scales for aggressiveness, extroversion, risk taking and need for collaboration. It doesn't mean you have to match perfectly, but someone with high self-awareness can relate in a broad variety of environments. Those who don't understand themselves attempt to be chameleons.

15. Talk too much. The best way to sell yourself is to be interested, ask good questions, be a good listener. They are trying to get to know you and you are trying to understand more about them. Take good advantage of their time and willingness to share information. That means answering concisely; make your key points but don't overelaborate. Assume that they will ask for detail where they want it.

16. Say bad things about anyone. You never know who is connected to whom. Remember everyone in the world is connected to everyone else by no more than three or four linkages. Your mother was right, "If you haven't got something nice to say, don't say it." You can throw the entire interview away if you take a pot-shot at some public figure who turns out to be the best friend of your interviewer.

Eight Ways to Say You're Not Interested and Have Them Come Back for More

You have the "no" card, your power to let the process unfold naturally and yet feel that you don't have to go along with things you don't want.

But the important thing to remember is that, when you want out, play the "no" card quickly, and play it with finesse. People can accept the "no" as long as they don't feel that you have held out until long after you knew the answer yourself. The graciousness comes in expressing your reason in a way that is not a negative reflection on the people you have met. You also don't want your reason to become part of a permanent profile that then excludes you from other similar opportunities. The trick is expressing your reasons in ways that aren't necessarily permanent. Make the client feel that he wasn't rejected. Say that, under other circumstances, you would have been honored.

There is a ritual and convention to this. Just to have some fun, let's list the eight ways to say no nicely—and what everyone knows they really mean,

1. "I feel an obligation to finish some things I have started here." Translation: "Many of the things you are offering me are going to happen to me where I am anyway."

2. "I am not a certain enough candidate for it to be worthwhile for you to spend time on me at this point." Translation: "Surprise me." This is saying no, "unless there is something about this job that I don't understand in terms of upsides, etc."

3. "Too much of what this job entails is repetition for me. I am eager to do different kinds of things." Translation: "You've got to be kidding. This is a lateral move."

4. "I have never thought about these kinds of jobs before. I am pretty focused on the tasks I am doing. Maybe I ought to have my eyes wide open but this is a little too far afield for me right now." Translation: "I wouldn't mind seeing other things like this and maybe relatively soon, but this isn't the one."

5. "I like everything I hear about your client and over time I would love to think about being part of that organization." Translation: "It is a great company but this isn't a big enough job. I don't want to be presumptuous, so I just hope that we either stay in touch or this job can be enlarged over time."

6. "I am potentially interested but I have some spouse and family issues that ultimately I would have to be address." This is always a dangerous one. What you are really saying is "I would like to

learn more but I can't even give you a firm yes or no about my level of interest." The client will rightfully say, "Look, those issues should be the ones most obvious from the get go. If they are big, let's be honest about it and not use them as a reason to back away." On one hand it is legitimate not to expect families to go through trauma when there is ultimately no decision to be made, so it is still a good way to delay making a commitment without necessarily giving a categorical rejection. Most search consultants will tell you that when a spouse or family issue is raised, it is very iffy, at best, whether the candidate will accept the offer and ultimately move. Most executives already understand what circumstances and geography are acceptable to their families and are preparing to say no in a way that they feel is less "insulting."

7. "This is something that might make sense at another stage in my career but not now." This is a nice "two-for." It means you need to hit it bigger before something like this can be considered. It is the usual response to public sector, government, not-for-profit or prestigious yet low-paying jobs. It says, "I would be interested in those over time, but help me find the big payday in the meantime."

8. "Over time I want the freedom to do things where money isn't the issue." Translation: "Right now money is the issue. I need to see equity and upsides that aren't apparent in this situation."

There is an art to saying no and being asked again. There is no limit to the number of times you can say no as long as you are consistent in your position and polite in your phrasing.

PART THREE

Tales from the Front

The Search Firm's Partners Speak

Beyond collecting the ranking of selection factors, I had the opportunity to survey the search firm's partners about a variety of issues that go beyond just data. In each case we began with their written comments to "open-ended" questions and then had one-on-one follow-up interviews.

In the first chapter in this section, we asked the search firm partners to boil down what they had seen during their experience that would help us get a sense of the most important executive selection factors. We asked, "If you could only know one or two things about a candidate, what would they be?" Experts who do studies call this a forced ranking technique, and it offsets the tendency people have to list a large number of factors. It helped us distill out those criteria on which the true discriminations are made.

We also asked them to look at the other side of the equation. We asked, "Where are the risks and pitfalls?" We asked them to describe the worst disaster they ever saw of a candidate eliminating himself from contention. This also was a forced ranking to get at those faux pas that are unrecoverable.

In Chapter 9, we asked them to turn the tables and talk to their own clients. How do they advise a company to be a smart user of search services? All our partners had strong views. They want their clients to be better clients, recognizing that the better a client is the more likely it will be happy with the outcome. There was also some frustration in handling difficult clients. They had a number of very telling insights and were eager to contribute them.

All in all, our partners said they enjoyed the opportunity to talk candidly in a way that sometimes isn't possible when they are actually on an engagement. For example, many said they avoid coaching candidates so as not to create favoritism or influence the results. But without the constraints of a specific assignment they had plenty of useful things to say. I hope you enjoy their comments.

What Search Firms' Partners Want to Know

If They Could Know Only One or Two Things about a Candidate

Introduction

Not surprisingly, most of what the search firms' partners wanted to know about candidates are the items at the top of the criteria in the specifications and finalist stages. It was interesting when they were asked to pick just one or two of these. And it was enlightening to hear their descriptions of both what they really want to understand and how they go about reaching that understanding. This kind of forced ranking requires respondents to identify those issues that they *really* use to discriminate between candidates. It turns out that only five different questions made the cut.

What Was The Value Added?

This was by far the most important thing they wanted to know. What did the candidate do to help achieve the company's goals over and above what would have happened under natural market conditions?

The responses had two dimensions. One was the "over and above" natural market conditions. Companies and areas of responsibility have a certain natural momentum that occurs regardless of the input from the leadership. It was most useful to determine the degree to which the candidate had successfully altered that natural momentum for the good. That is the economic value added.

The other dimension concerns the relatively high inertia built into organizations and how managers receive both too much credit for good things and too much blame for bad things that were already in process when their tenure began. Warren Buffet's famous quote reflects this point: "When a manager with a reputation for being brilliant encounters an industry with the reputation for being difficult, it will be the reputation of the industry that survives." The partners said that understanding what *specific* role the candidates really played in successes is one of the most difficult things to ascertain.

Not only do you have to understand how much momentum was already in place, you have to unscramble the personal contributions. Were the results due to implementation by the candidate or because of strategic or investment decisions made by others at different places and different times? One partner said, "All the resume tells you is where they were in broad brush strokes. It tells you very little about what was going during those periods and almost nothing about what the individual's contribution was." This is vital information pulled from discussion, research and reference checking. That is why it is the most important thing to get your hands on.

What Happens When the Pressure Is On?

In second place was understanding how candidates are likely to behave when they are not on their best behavior. Our partners said this in a variety of ways. They wanted to know how the candidates responded to deadlines. They want to understand what critical skills the candidates use when the task is urgent. Do they become more dictatorial or less communicative? How do they handle the heat? The search firm's partners talked about asking questions that require the candidate to describe how she handles ambiguity, which is another form of pressure that tempts people back to their natural mode.

How Does the Candidate "Wear and Fit" over the Long Haul?

Most people can make themselves fit into a situation either when the pressure is on or when they are being observed for a short period. But over the long haul, like married couples who grow irritated over differences about how to squeeze the toothpaste, the cultural fit can chafe as people revert to type. The partners said they would love to understand how the candidates achieved their results, and they wanted to look underneath the public track record. Did the candidate use a style that the organization respected and admired or did she achieve results in spite of a style that people find difficult over time? They wanted to understand whether the person was a doer, a coach or a counselor. They wanted to know whether the candidate was a professional manager and delegator, or a craftsman who led by technical expertise.

How Strategically Does the Person's Mind Work?

We are back again to the major characteristics. Our partners said they wanted to understand the person's ability and inclination to think strategically rather than tactically. How much skill did he have as a long-range planner? How visionary was he? Over what time frames did he tend to think and believe he had responsibility and accountability? What was the mix between his strategic skills and his implementation skills? The partners said they tried to let the candidates talk about accomplishments and their situation analyses as a way of identifying which factors the candidate focused on and which perspectives he brought to a problem.

If the Job Is Offered, How Likely Is She to Move Ahead?

The search firm's partners wanted to understand whether the person was a realistic candidate, someone who was likely to move under the right circumstances as opposed to someone just taking an ego massage or window shopping. They refer to this as trying to understand the push–pull factors. How much of the candidate's interest comes from the fact that she feels pushed in her current situation versus how much attraction the prospective job exerts? One of the search consultants said, "The stronger the push, the less the pull has to be, but then it becomes important to understand if any of the reasons for the push bother you in terms of the candidate's profile." That means understanding why the candidate wants the job. Is it the attraction per se or the opportunity to get out of a situation where she is blocked or frustrated? Others refer to this as the "close-ability" factor (i.e., likelihood the deal will close). This means understanding the candidate's decision-making models, how he looks at the size of the job, what the job would do to his career pattern, the compensation and related opportunities, geographical issues, size of company issues and family issues.

We talked about how candidates should discuss their degree of interest. The consensus of advice was to be honest and timely. Candidates shouldn't feel that they need to express higher interest than required to stay in the game. The "I don't know" or "I need to find out more" responses are perfectly acceptable. On the other hand, the best candidates will also confirm their interest as it increases or express themselves clearly when their interest wanes.

The Worst Disaster I Ever Saw

"Disaster" is a relative term. To get on search firms' radar for senior executive jobs, candidates have already been vetted and tested over a long time and by many people. These people are not ignorant of the process. These people are not ignorant of how they are being judged, nor are they unskilled in handling themselves under a variety of testing circumstances. Most of our partners said that they don't see terrible disasters too often. But every one had at least one or two disaster stories, situations in which people who seemed to have everything going for them shot themselves in the foot. These lessons are important.

Mortal Sin Number One: Embellishing Education, Degrees, Job Roles, Titles or Compensation

Without exception, the worst disasters all tended to fall in this category. These were people who buffed up their resume with things that were just not true. And the saddest fact, in almost all cases, was that the unembellished resume would have been more than adequate, given the person's record of accomplishments.

It is not that the reasons aren't understandable. In one case, a female candidate for the presidency of a division had all the right skills and experiences. As the reference checking began, it was discovered she had listed both bachelor's and master's degrees, yet had neither. The actual story was that, married right out of college, she had dropped out just short of her degree. Several years later, when the marriage dissolved and she needed work, she "completed" her degree and added a fictitious MBA to get her foot in the door. All her subsequent accomplishments were consistent with someone who had these degrees. In this case the good news was that the hiring managers made an exception and understood the circumstances. But in most cases, the discovery of an untruth, regardless of how good or how minor the reason, becomes a disqualifying event. In a similar case with two candidates, the preferred choice continued to duck providing her Social Security number. It became clear that she understood that her Social Security number was required to conduct degree verification. Earlier in her career, to earn more and crack into a more professional job, she had fabricated her degree. The company felt since she wasn't able to own up to them, she couldn't be trusted and lost the opportunity.

In another case, a senior attorney considered for a chief adminis-trative job backed himself into a corner by lying about his salary. As the process progressed, the person's compensation level was not a par-ticular issue. But by then, the candidate was so far into denial about the fact that he had misrepresented his earnings record that, when he presented a W2 form to confirm his compensation history, he claimed the government's records were inaccurate. Another case involved a candidate who claimed on his resume that, early in his career, he had worked in a well-known company's program that tar-geted high-performing people who then spent a year as the chair-man's special executive assistant. All of his subsequent assignments and accomplishments were consistent with the caliber of people who had done it. In fact, he was never part of the program. That one falsehood threw him out of contention not only for that job but for other future possibilities.

Omitting a Job or "Papering Over" a Resume Gap

The reasons are understandable. A candidate makes a mistake, is down-sized, outplaced, and hides or camouflages the fact in the resume chronology. In a presidential search that one of the partners handled, a candidate was made a verbal offer contingent on reference checking. As it turns out, someone in the company helping with the reference checking remembered him working for a company not listed on the resume. When they called that company, it was verified that he was there for a short period. The candidate replied, "Well, it was just five or six months. I got there; it was a disaster. They had misrepresented what the job was and so I just pulled out and started over. I didn't think it was worth making a big statement about in the grand sweep of things." The company pulled the offer.

Resume gaps are more common and more complex today. The stigma of having been fired or outplaced by mergers no longer exists. But search firms and their client companies expect candor when these points are examined in detail. That is not to say that you need to spell out that for four months you were looking for a job or on an out-placement program. But most of the partners said the smart thing to do is construct your resume so that it shows the main accomplishments, and then in the discussion with the search partners handle the transition points with accuracy and full disclosure. There should never be any subsequent embarrassing information that comes to light later.

Getting Ahead of the Process

Earlier we talked about how candidates must not rush the process. The third category of disaster our partners talked about were those cases where the candidate didn't follow that rule. One partner described a case where a CEO candidate was being interviewed by the nonexec-utive chairman of the board. In the very first interview, the candidate asked the chairman how long he was going to be in that position and if he could secure guarantees that he, the candidate, would succeed to that chair in a timely fashion. That was a topic only to be discussed as and when the company determined its first choice. The candidate's impatience with the question and focus on that issue ended the possibility of what might otherwise have been a good fit.

In a similar case, a search was on for a division president. They wanted someone who was expected to grow the business from $300 or $400 million to about $1 billion. In the eyes of the search firm partners, they had the perfect candidate. He had impressed everyone he met, all the way up the line. In his first interview with the chairman, the candidate's opening statement was that he wouldn't consider moving for that particular job. It was interpreted as a direct confrontation with the company's president, who had the next job in the hierarchy. The candidate said that he liked to drop bombshells to see how people react. Over time, the division presidency was certainly a stepping-stone job to the number two position in the company. But the company viewed it as their prerogative to open that line of discussion. He was dropped from consideration.

SEARCH FIRM SECRETS

Every Search Has the Same Rhythm (and You Can't Negotiate before Phase Four)

✓ Let's look for ourselves.

✓ Do we like him or her?

✓ Does he or she like us?

✓ The object of our affection.

The search firm's partners mentioned other disasters of "the wrong thing at the wrong time" type; these included people who couldn't wait to focus on retirement or bonus plan details. Or candidates who wanted assurances that this would involve at least an X percent increase before they would have any more conversations. Again, the sophisticated candidate understands that the search firm and the client do not expect any candidate to make a change that isn't in his or her best interest. It is insulting to assume that they need to be grilled on whether they have done their homework on that subject.

When the True Colors Show Through

Some candidates, either though fatigue or lack of understanding, blew off certain interviews with junior people. They treated their discussions or interactions with lower-level people as irrelevant and emitted an attitude of, "Why do I need to visit with you?" or "Why have they bothered to take up my time with somebody like you?" Other candidates were disqualified when it became clear that visions of grandeur appeared as they became more confident about being the prime candidate. In one case, when the candidate was told that the company would be making him a formal offer shortly, he asked to see the best offices in the company's headquarters regardless of whether they were currently occupied. That turned off so many people that the offer was never made.

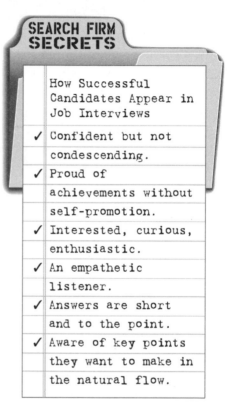

SEARCH FIRM SECRETS

How Successful Candidates Appear in Job Interviews

✓ Confident but not condescending.

✓ Proud of achievements without self-promotion.

✓ Interested, curious, enthusiastic.

✓ An empathetic listener.

✓ Answers are short and to the point.

✓ Aware of key points they want to make in the natural flow.

In other cases, it takes longer for that kind of thing to show up. One of the search firm's partners described a case where the client felt very good about one candidate, even though the partner had reservations and told the client that he didn't think the person was pursuing the job for the right reasons. As it turned out, the candidate took the job, but was fired 30 days later when he directed that $30,000 worth of the client company's products be installed at his home.

If You Can't Say Something Nice, Don't Say Anything

A number of disasters related to denigrating the candidate's current company or individuals within it, betraying confidences or telling stories out of school. One of our partners said it may be true that your boss is a moron, that the other inside candidate you are competing with for the CEO's job is a liar and a cheat, or that your current company is headed to hell in a handbasket. But none of those perspectives ought to be shared.

Minor Disasters Are Reversible

A number of clients stressed that minor disasters, if handled with grace and good humor, don't interfere with the process and can sometimes enhance it. It is only if the candidate is so nervous and uptight that he turns a minor disaster into a major issue that causes the big problem. One partner cited the case of a candidate who was about to be offered the job and was flying to three different cities to visit the company's key directors. Unfortunately, his wife had taken the wrong suit jacket to the cleaners so that when he grabbed what he assumed was a fresh suit from the cleaner's bag, it mismatched his trousers. Given the choice of blowing off the trip, trying to rent a suit, or saying the luggage was lost, or telling the truth, everyone was impressed that the candidate took it calmly. He called the directors on his schedule and told them what had happened and asked whether they would mind if he arrived carrying his suit jacket over his arm for their visit. Everyone was impressed with his style and self-confidence and it only enhanced their enthusiasm for him as a candidate.

People understand and respond to honesty and circumstances. It is the sense that they are being manipulated or treated without respect, rather then the actual omission or mistake, that gets people into trouble.

Disasters are avoidable because they all come from things under the candidates' control. If you tell the truth, be yourself, follow the golden rule and look at things through other peoples' eyes, you will have nothing to worry about.

Chapter 9

How to Be a Smart Client

Introduction: Both Sides Want the Same Thing

Unlike some kinds of client/agent relationships, a very powerful symmetry exists between the goals of the search firm and the goals of the client. This symmetry may not exist in other relationships the corporation encounters. For example, a corporation's investment banker gets paid only if the deal goes through or if the company gets sold. There is a strong incentive to do the deal, even if it is not necessarily in the client's interest. Legal firms getting paid by the hour may have incentives to make more out of a case than is necessarily in the client's interest. But these asymmetries don't color the relationship with search firms. The reality is this:

1. Both sides want an executive placed in the job who will ultimately be successful.

2. Both sides want an executive placed in the position who has long-term potential to take on even more responsibility with the client.

3. Both sides want the client to feel so satisfied that there are future search assignments given.

As we talked with our search firm's partners, however, it became clear that there is a wide continuum in terms of how successful companies get the most out of these relationships. There was a frustration that not everyone takes advantage of this symmetry. To a person, their frustration was not with the smart client who does what it takes to get and demand the best, but with the client who doesn't take full advantage of the partnership. What then do our partners say it takes to demand the best? What does it take on the client's part to maximize the return?

Start with Goals and Strategies, Not Specifications

Every partner we talked to said the same thing. First, have the *search firm* do the job description. Clients who draft the specifications themselves ignore the search firm's expertise at the most vital stage, which involves understanding the link between what the client wants to accomplish and the kind of person it will take to achieve those accomplishments. I asked the partners why this occurred. Some said they thought it stemmed from an attitude on the client's part that "we know this business, therefore we know what it takes to do these jobs." Others said they thought that companies worried that the search firm would set the specs too broadly so it would be easier to find qualifying candidates. Others said that, in many cases, the job already existed, so some form of description and spec sheet also already existed.

The best way to create the specs is start from scratch and begin with the goals. The company should talk with the search firm about current circumstances and what the successful incumbent should end up accomplishing. Having the search firm draft the position specifications ensures they understand the critical issues. It is also the best way to make sure they understand the relative importance of various factors.

Have the Search Firm Help You Avoid Hiring in Your Own Image

The search firm is in the best position to help you hire what you need, as opposed to what you already have. This is where the cultural balancing act we discussed in Chapter 6 takes place. When executives develop the specifications on their own, they conclude that a person who looks just like them is the right model for success. But the search firm knows who is out there, and the search firm has a broad experience base by which to judge what kind of profile it takes to achieve the goals the client wants. The search firm also brings the objectivity necessary to know whether more of the same is needed, or someone who adds a new dimension.

Be Candid about the Problems, Issues and Challenges

The smart clients are those who make sure there is full disclosure of all the issues immediately. If a job went to a search firm, it is often because there was an unsatisfactory end to the previous incumbent's tenure or that person retired and left no successor. The incumbent may have moved on before the organization matured or there may have been a battle for succession that created friction within the organization. Whatever the reasons, it is clear that any good candidate will discover this information. Since it will come out anyway, it is better to deal with it up front. Not only does this give the search firm all the information it needs to understand the kind of candidate and skills they should be looking for, but it puts them in the best position to make a full presentation.

Have All Subsequent Discoveries by the Candidates Be Positive

Clients are tempted to say, "Wait a second, I don't need to share all of this dirty laundry with a bunch of strangers. Shouldn't we just wait until we get our finalists and then bring them in on the full picture?" No one is making the case to have this kind of information be part of the job specs or the initial phone calls with prospects and sources. But the search partners need to know what is going on from the beginning. As viable candidates emerge, they need to be briefed before doing any extensive visiting with executives. People at this level will feel manipulated if they are allowed to go into interviews blind to the real issues and dynamics. Willing and appropriate candidates will be lost by the implicit assumption that they can't be trusted with the entire perspective in order to make up their minds about the situation. On the other hand, if you get the tough issues disclosed early, then you'll be setting the stage that builds toward the candidate's enthusiastic agreement to join your firm.

Invest in Having the Search Firm Get to Know You Beyond the Immediate Position

Also at the top of the list was the demand that the search firm spend enough time up-front with a broad cross section of people in the firm. This ensures they have an important understanding of the cultural context. Have them *visit* with peers of the open position and other key positions involved with the hiring manager. The search firm partner should understand the personalities with whom the prospective executive must work, and understand the organization's quirks and peculiarities. He then can provide candidates with a more accurate description and assessment. This allows candidates to be more precise about their level of interest sooner, and consequently moves the process ahead more efficiently.

Sometimes this approach creates conflict with senior HR executives. They may perceive that their job is to insulate the managers from search firms so as not to waste the managers' time or create distraction. But the smart HR executives know when to play gatekeeper. They know that when it comes to handling the logistical parts of the search assignment, they should insist that the search partner deal through them. But where the purpose is to get a cross section of perspective on the job and the issues at the front end, the HR executives and search partner should understand they have the same goals. They both want to ensure that the search partner gets enough up-front interactions so the search firm is not looking in the wrong direction.

Help the Search Firm Sell Your Firm to Candidates

Once the search firm partner has learned the advantages of the firm, its strengths and the reason why people enjoy working there, he can sell it better. Not only can the search firm partner better answer candidates' questions, but he can extol the positive attitude transmitted by those who have been successful within the firm. Often the most important questions a search partner can ask of people beyond the hiring manager is not related to the specific job but are questions such as, "What is it that you find appealing about working at this firm?" "What characteristics make people feel that the firm will continue to be successful?" At the end of day, the most successful clients see the search firm as their partner in "selling" candidates. The best candidates are people who didn't apply for the job, but need to discover its attractions.

The Partnership During the Search

It is telling of the successful client firm that so many activities take place before the search itself technically begins. This front-end work and long-term orientation separate those who get the most out of these relationships from those who don't. Soon enough you hit the point where the goals are understood and specs written; the search firm has a broad understanding of the job and the cultural setting and it's time to start talking to people. There are five points our partners say characterize the smart clients during this active phase.

1. Smart clients take joint responsibility for the success of the search. They don't sit back and expect the search firm to simply serve up people, nor is their attitude that of "next . . . next . . . next . . . show me what else you've got." Some clients feel somehow that the search firm represents all those people out there who would like the job and if they just wait long enough the search firm will bring the best ones forward. But the search firm represents you and it can only do its best job when you take an active role.

2. Smart clients give the partners timely, in-depth feedback about each candidate; such feedback helps refine and retarget the search. Conversely, if the feedback is delayed, you will get the search firm continuing to look for the same profile. Saying, "We are not impressed with that one, let's see another" is the same as giving no feedback. Some clients either allow or require that the search firm partner sit in on the initial company interviews with the first one or two candidates. When the feedback comes, they have the specifics of how the interview went. This lets them calibrate whether the feedback is specific to the candidate and how she handled the interview or represented a more generic company issue.

3. Smart clients do not let candidates dangle. Once someone has been identified, the client must interview the person fairly soon. It fosters a terrible impression if someone is approached after

the initial interview with a search firm and is told that the client would like to see them, yet it takes four or five weeks to arrange it. The client sends the signal that either you are not a high-priority candidate or the firm is disorganized, and neither may be true.

4. After the candidate has been interviewed, and the client has provided quick and candid feedback, the client should make a yes/no determination. If all candidates are kept in some sort of backup queue, the feedback is muddy and the search firm doesn't understand how many more candidates it needs to present. Without pressing to yes/no status, a search firm can believe it is closing in after having presented three or four candidates, only to have the client say, "Well, none of them are really any good." You lose much time if the search firm starts to wind down and then must gear back up.

5. Finally, it is important during the active phase of the search to focus and refocus on the two or three key skills most urgently required. There is always a risk that the sorting gets done based on minor or extraneous factors. Not everyone who speaks with a candidate may understand the big picture or, in fact, be a great interviewer. The manager responsible should focus on the cultural fit and the two or three other absolutely necessary skills. It is too easy to hang on to someone who, although likable, friendly or attractive, is missing three of the four key requirements. Similarly, it is important to put minor negatives in perspective. Significant candidates should not be disqualified over secondary characteristics or a minor aspect of cultural fit. A candidate who had four great interviews, but also one that was a bit off, is likely to be better than one who had five "good but not great" interviews with no dissent—but no great enthusiasm either.

The Smartest Companies Use the Search Firm as a Source of Competitive Intelligence Even When There Is No Current Search Going On

This is an area where I heard frustration in the partners' comments. They said, "We know what's out there, and we can be part of your competitive radar even when there is no search going on. We want to be used and we want to contribute."

More search firms are moving toward an industry specialization and they are out in the relevant market all the time. Smart clients bring them in periodically to talk about what is going on in the industry, what areas are hot for hiring, and what trends or key topics are emerging. They ask whether they see people moving in certain predictable patterns and whether there is a consensus on the leading edge issues. But if you don't ask and don't make arrangements to take advantage of this market intelligence, you won't get it. And that is your substantial loss.

What to Demand

Smart clients make expectations clear up front. They do their own homework on the firm to make sure it has the expertise and appropriate specialty for the task. They check out whether it has the reach or is blocked in too many significant areas. But most importantly, smart clients understand who will be executing the work. They understand the role of the search firm partner with whom they are having the dialogue. They understand the background and expertise of the research team and whether execution partners or principals will be involved and, if so, what their role is to be.

They should also set explicit ground rules on the conduct of the search. At the client firm, the person responsible for the engagement should have an absolute assurance as to how often he and the partner on the search will visit. They should have clear guidelines for how long it will take to develop the position specifications. They should agree how soon they receive background material to review after potential candidates have been interviewed by the search firm.

In all ways, expectations should be for high responsiveness and great candor on both sides. The search firms should be invited to comment on the specs and how realistic the profile and compensation dimensions are relative to the market. The role of the HR department must be spelled out clearly. When are they to be the point of contact, and when and under what circumstances should the search firm provide feedback directly to the person responsible for the engagement?

The smart firm and its search firm partner are also clear about what happens if they can't attract any of the top two or three candidates. Most firms have policies on what happens if a placed candidate either quits or fails to meet expectations within the first six months or year. Those should be understood by both sides.

How to Select a Firm

In the final analysis, this is a still a partnership where chemistry is key. Start with a search firm that knows you best, and who can tell your firm's story most effectively. You need someone who understands the cultural fit issue well and in whose judgment you have confidence. You also then need to consider the question of industry expertise. Is this a search where industry expertise is critically important, and does the person you are working with in the firm bring that to the table? This is important. You want both the firm and the partner to have the appropriate base of knowledge and contacts. But you also need to understand the "off limits" cases. Search firms normally cannot solicit an executive from a company or division they have served in the last two or three years. Industry experience may be of little practical benefit if, by using that search firm, you wall yourself off from too many companies where talent is likely to be found.

While it is often important for your firm to have industry expertise, you also want to factor in how important it is to have global reach. Today, many of the leading firms have global affiliations so they can both source and identify and then contact candidates from other areas. Since the ideal situation for the client is developing a long-term relationship where you have invested a significant amount of time and energy to bring the search firm to a solid understanding of you and your issues, you want to make sure that they have the capabilities to handle your requirements on the same scale as your ambitions and opportunities.

Finally, you want to understand the degree of sophistication that the search firm brings in terms of databases and research capabilities. These days, your potential candidates could be anywhere in the world with any number of global competitors or comparable firms. You want to be sure that your partner has the ability to identify those who fit the profile regardless of where they are or where they might currently be working.

The reality is that essentially all of the major-name search firms meet these criteria. The differences between Heidrick & Struggles; Korn, Ferry; Russell Reynolds; Spencer Stuart; and Ray and Berndtson aren't in the degree of industry expertise. They all have it with some modest differences in mix and depth. The differences aren't in the area of global reach since they are all capable of operating around the world. And it isn't in the sophistication of info systems or research. In the final analysis, these firms can be differentiated by the degree of comfort the client feels about the people who will be working with you and executing your business. Choose those who understand what it takes to be successful and who understand how to work with you to make you the smartest client you can be.

Conclusion

Search firm partners really won't say so, but they actually see clients in two classes. In group one are the clients who stand back from the process. They see search firms as "name collectors." They see candidates as applicants who are trying to sell themselves to the client. But the truth is these people are limiting their opportunities and getting less out of the relationships than could be the case if they were willing to work a little harder and a little smarter.

The second group is the smart clients. Search partners see smart clients as those who treat the search firm as partners and view them as a source of competitive intelligence and long-term understanding even when there is no immediate search going on. They understand that their job is working with the search firm to find the best talent available. And that means accessing the people who aren't easy to find or aren't aggressively looking. And that their job together is to take an accurate but motivating vision of the client's opportunity forward and engage the kind of people whose talent can make that vision into a reality. These are the clients that are the most fun to work with even if they are more demanding. They are the ones that take more time but where the results make both parties feel good about the partnership.

PART FOUR

The Book of Lists

This next section sorts the secrets into checklists based on age and situation. Executives on the move understand that they are competing with and compared to their peers. The norms are different for different peer groups. No one expects a 28-year-old product manager to have the same profile as a 36-year old division manager. But if the 28-year-old lags his or her own peer group, not much else will convince a search firm that person is worth tracking.

But there is another standard against which all executive candidates are compared that is not so obvious. It is the current version of the "mythic manager." Today, with so many "how to" books on management, there is a vague sense of the ideal manager that exists in the public consciousness, even if no one person can live up to this ideal. Managers on the move may not subscribe to these managerial fads and models, but they should certainly understand them, since the people who will be interviewing them have these images as part of their standard of comparison.

Not only are these assumptions about the mythic manager unspoken, they change with time. So, before we expose you to the checklists that apply to peer groups, let's provide a longer-term perspective on the public image of the ideal manager.

Chapter 10

Unspoken Assumptions

Evolution of the Mythic Manager

The Search for the Magic Bullet

The notion of managing as a profession is a modern one. In the 1700s and 1800s, people were said to be "in business," but it was presumed that it was the "doing" of the trade or craft that was the key skill. Much of the world's work was done in the individual proprietorship, on family farms or in cottage industries. There were businesspeople, but there was little notion of "managing" as a separate skill. The most successful businesspeople were industrialists, financiers or merchants. There were politicians and generals who provided leadership, but it wasn't until the early 1900s where the skill of management was acknowledged as being distinct from the skills involved in product creation.

It is not surprising that the first theories of high-performing management in the early 1900s were engineering models—based on mass production and the assembly line. People said that the successful manager was one who could look at the production process and engineer a different design for the big machine that constituted the company's organization for manufacturing.

At the same time, Gilbreth, Taylor and others were pioneers in time and motion studies. In both cases the fundamental view was that of something similar to physics or chemistry. The theory was that if you could break the process down into its smallest components, there were certain immutable laws that must be followed. The "chemical" reactions would then occur at the same time and in the same way as long as the ingredients were mixed in the right proportions.

Inherent in this view, of course, is an assumption about workers that is not particularly complimentary. It assumes that the best way to improve their productivity is to train them in the narrowest range of activities and ask them to repeat them over and over at relatively high volumes. Any acknowledgment of the ability to think, reason, or judge was only in a negative sense. These faculties were assumed to be the sources of imperfections and distractions. These distractions could only be bred out of the process by standardization and focus on the subdivision of work into small, easily repeated pieces.

Organizations that adopted this approach enjoyed substantial initial productivity gains compared to individual assembly. Ultimately, as the production process became more complex, the price of ignoring human factors showed up and was manifested in worker dissatisfaction and alienation. Where worker dissatisfaction was prevalent, quality and productivity both declined. The mass production approach and the time and motion study approach provided no clues and no solutions for repairing processes that gradually grew out of control, unhinged by what was inadequate attention to the human dimensions.

The 1940s and 1950s models of successful management were dominated by experiences that came out of World War II. Superior logistical management was considered key at this time, and success came from commandeering resources and applying overwhelming force at key points during designated times. This school of thought postulated that a leader created a command-and-control organization where a relatively small number of people with superior analytic thinking skills exercised precise control over the flow of resources and the tasks of individuals. The "Whiz Kids" of Ford in the 1950s were literally the same people who had brought quantitative measurement and control systems to bear on the resources necessary to win the war. It was presumed that this was the prototype of the successful general manager. This person would bring high analytic wizardry to the job and oversee the application of sophisticated financial controls. The underlying assumption about the workforce in the Whiz Kids model did not take much more notice of human factors than did the assembly line.

But the Whiz Kid model requires a management hierarchy. Since the Whiz Kids believed their job was to create financial and control systems, they needed a relatively broad organization of middle and upper-middle managers performing functional tasks of engineering, marketing and production. In WWII, the traditionally autonomous field commanders and generals were made part of even bigger organizations called "theaters" or "the supreme allied command." This approach created the conviction that organizations could become bigger and bigger as long as there was an adequate hierarchy and a system of financial controls. It was assumed that the key job of management was to provide that infrastructure. By the 1950s, these assumptions were behind the huge growth of the industrial giants in autos, steel, industrial products and petroleum.

By the 1960s, the success of the industrial giants provided the impetus for the first generation of conglomerates. Conglomerate CEOs were epitomized by Harold Geneen at ITT. Geneen believed in having a broad variety of companies (portfolio diversification) and then managing the managers of those portfolio companies with a combination of tight controls, financial reporting and intimidation. In hindsight, the successes attributed to these management philosophies are likely to have been substantially the product of the post-war U.S. monopoly on key products and technologies. Costs were essentially irrelevant since we could—and did—charge whatever it cost to make cars, steel, airplanes, locomotives and TVs. Tapping the ingenuity of production workers to improve productivity and flexibility wasn't a factor in this equation.

By the late 1950s and early 1960s, management was becoming more accepted as not only a profession but as a field worthy of study and research. The nation's business schools reached their first level of maturity. The financial and control experts, and time and motion experts, were joined by a new class of academician and research consultant from the behavioral and humanities side. Business was being studied as a science. These new business scientists assumed there were high level strategies that could be brought to bear to produce better results. Both groups (the engineer/strategists and the behaviorists) began to look for the "magic bullets." To the engineers/strategists, the most important job the CEO did was to find the optimum strategy. The behaviorists believed that success was a function of creating the right corporate structure and incentives. To them, the CEO's job consisted of building environments that would motivate people and "shape" their behaviors.

The strategists were exemplified by the work done by General Electric and SRI on the profit impact of market share. Widely known as the PIMS Study, this was an enormous data analysis of companies, their profitability and the profit margins of their products. It concluded that the most important role of the CEO was to adopt a strategy for the company to become the market-share leader for its industry. All good things would flow from that market share leadership. Later, it became clear that, while market share and a number of other positive financial results were linked, one was not the cause of the other. Today, we suspect today that high market share and high profits might both be products of a third set of conditions. But 30 years ago, this mind-set led to the Boston Consulting Group and others to focus on the "learning curve" as being the key to all financial success. The premise was that if you had higher total cumulative output than your competition, you would have a lower unit cost. It led to the famous "two-by-two" grid in which companies sorted all of their product lines and divisions into "stars," "cash cows" and "dogs." Management was reduced to three relatively straightforward orientations: focus on market share; focus on where you are on the learning curve; focus on creating a portfolio of "cash-using" and "cash-eating" businesses—and then sit back and enjoy the benefits.

Research conducted by behaviorists during this same time assumed that the performance of human beings throughout the organization was as important as the strategy decisions made at the top. They assumed the real challenge for management was to engage the entire organization in positive and productive behavior. In 1966, Frederick Herzberg published his seminal book, *Work and the Nature of Man*. It argued that managers needed to understand that their principal task was to motivate the human beings within their organizations to higher levels of productivity, and he offered a specific formula. Herzberg argued that what he called the hygiene factors (working conditions, i.e., compensation, corporate policies, etc.) were not capable of achieving positive worker satisfaction. These factors were only capable of either increasing or decreasing degrees of *dissatisfaction*. Herzberg's point was that only the factors intrinsic to the job itself—a sense of accomplishment, a sense of doing something worthwhile, the challenge of excellence and the opportunity to achieve—created and spurred satisfaction. Only by engaging these higher levels of human needs were you able to tap into their potential to make increased contributions.

Until Herzberg, American managers, if they thought at all about the effect of worker satisfaction on worker motivation it was in terms of working conditions, not intellectual change. In reality, a substantial part of today's American management thinking has its roots in Herzberg. Today we talk about TQM, employee involvement groups and re-engineering, and we think them totally modern phenomenon. And yet, when one looks back to the 1960s and 1970s, when the buzzword was "quality of work life," we find many of the same basic components. The idea was that, by improving working conditions, managers could increase satisfaction, motivation and performance. Herzberg's work was central to this idea, because he was the first to highlight the importance of extrinsic factors, an idea later expanded by researchers who investigated defects of job design on worker performance.

Modern studies of high performance companies reinforce the presumption that the major advantage comes from tapping into what Herzberg terms the "Abraham" side of humans, the part that adheres to values and seeks achievement. Conversely, the best employers can do if they pay primary attention to the "Adam" side of human nature, i.e., the pain-avoidance and animal-needs part of our nature, is to reduce the potential for *dissatisfaction*. This probably affects only those negative factors like turnover, absenteeism and sabotage.

B. F. Skinner and other behavioralists assumed that the role of the manager is to focus on changing the behavior of workers in ways useful to the organization. Skinner advocated positive feedback in response to desired behavior. Negative feedback is of no use in achieving results, he claimed. So experienced managers would identify the results wanted and ensure that the behaviors that accomplished this were reinforced. As desired results became more frequent, less reinforcement was needed.

By the 1980s, the competition between the "strategists" and "structuralists" had evolved to where it was taken up by nonacademic popularizers. These popularizers could, in turn, be characterized as being either "simplifiers" or "complicators." The most popular of the behaviorally-oriented management gurus of the 1980s tended to be simplifiers. Books like *The One Minute Manager* and *In Search of Excellence* took the psychological underpinnings of the structuralists and translated them into a handful of key pieces of advice. This led to such buzzwords (or buzzphrases) as "management by walking around," and the "one-minute praising," "one-minute feedback" schools of leadership.

On the strategy and "complicator" side, it became clear that if a little was good, more was better. Peter Drucker wrote huge tomes on the role of management. Michael Porter of Harvard Business School wrote a series of books on identifying sources of strategy and competitive advantage. Lester Thurow wrote extensively about comparative advantage. Consulting firms like McKinsey came up with no less than seven "S's" essential for managers to understand.

By the 1990s, both sides had surrendered to the sound bite. Gurus competed for attention with a series of "one-word" theme management doctrines. TQM, empowerment, vision, and reengineering were all shorthand that implied that all you needed was to understand *one* phrase, concept, or idea to become a truly exceptional manager.

Fortunately, the pendulum has swung back. In this second half of the 1990s, our understanding of high-performance management has become more sophisticated, with a clear understanding that no one size fits all. There is a better understanding that change is very difficult and staying on top is just as hard as getting there. Most of the buzzword fads ignored the fact that every decision you make sets off a chain reaction with which you must deal. Success in an organization undergoing change depends on the sequencing and understanding of contingencies. Organizations can only handle so much at one time.

Most managers do not have the time or inclination to wade through competing experimental results, and will continue initiating variations of the quality-of-work-life programs. All will be based, to some degree, on the assumption that increasing satisfaction increases performance. In today's "virtual" workplace, it is even more important to pay attention to the intrinsic factors of job performance and the motivating effects of achievement and pride of purpose. For the "work-at-home" employer and the member of the "virtual corporation," there is no *place* anymore in "workplace." This radical change creates another variable whose effect on the chemistry of human beings and organizational results is yet to be well understood.

Herzberg's important intuition drives much of today's management thinking. His argument that there should be two divisions of industrial relation has occurred. Human resource departments attend to the "hygiene factors," while line management creates achievement, growth and recognition factors for employees that will presumably increase productivity.

This duality is inherent in the conclusions of McKinsey's work on high-performing companies. McKinsey concluded that the productivity and performance leverage from empowering employees occurred only if a "spine" of certain values and practices were already in place. In fact, McKinsey found that the same kind of empowerment activities that enhance one company's productivity would lead to reductions in effectiveness in other companies where that performance-oriented culture was not already in place. Perhaps this is just repeating what Issac Newton observed—for every action there is an equal and opposite reaction. To build toward the heavens we need a foundation that will hold it all in place.

In the end, it becomes clear that much of the difference between a highly effective organization and one that isn't has little to do with strategy, positioning or technology. The winners are those with exceptional management skills. Our model of what a manager does has moved away from viewing people as machines or seeing management as some kind of engineering or physical science. It is now management's role to engage the entire human organization, to engage all facets of the individual personalities on both sides of the manager/employee line.

The principal lesson of the search firm files is that we *have* developed a sophisticated understanding of what it takes to be a great manager. We want people who understand technology, who understand the industry, who have had comparable positions, and have degrees from good schools. But the key skills reside in those senior executives who engage the whole of his or her organization on its human dimensions. This is why, for all industries, getting results is understood to be linked not to knowledge of business theories, but to skills—the ability to think strategically and then to engage others with that strategic vision. The most important managerial skill is knowing how to generate a vision people can embrace and will execute with enthusiasm. Without that linkage to the human side, management can accomplish very little. But with it there are no limits. *The Secrets from the Search Firm Files* can help future managers master this challenge, even given the amazing frustrations of being a leader.

Six Characteristics of High-Performing Companies (and They All Have to Do with Leadership)

This search for the magic bullet, for the unified field theory of management, still continues. The leading-edge work in academe and among the more sophisticated think-tanks and consulting organizations leads people to the same place. The factors that sort the best from the rest are not strategy or technology. They are the quality of leadership.

We understand now that it is an "execution" world. There are few protected positions, proprietary products, or lead times that amount to much, and there are no geographic or knowledge barriers you can hide behind for very long. With the cars all even and every one starting at the same place on the track, then it is the skill of the driver that matters. Earlier in this chapter there was a reference to a McKinsey & Company study that looked at a large number of public companies. The study singled out those that had generated exceptional total return to shareholders consistently over long periods and through a variety of business cycles. The study concluded that exceptional companies shared six broad characteristics, none of which had anything to do with specific strategies, technologies, size, market share or product. All six involved leadership skill and leadership will.

No summary can do justice to this kind of conceptual framework. Readers who are interested are referred to the *McKinsey Quarterly*, 1995, number 3. In summary, the work concluded that during extended periods of high performance the companies that achieved exceptional results all exhibited six similar attributes.

1. They were driven by leaders. No inertia or self-perpetuating process maintained their advantage. The leaders of these companies were demanding, "unreasonable" in the sense they set goals well above the logical extrapolation of current trends. They imbued the company with the conviction and sense of urgency to achieve goals not readily seen within the current range of capabilities. But these leaders were also able to contribute to the specifics of the business—they were not just generalists. They brought insight, intuition and experience to their organizations, and instilled a productive fear of failure. However, people were not afraid to take risks, but leadership created a sense that complacency was an enemy as perilous as competition. Even when things were going well, the leadership questioned what conditions might challenge their supremacy, and would take preemptive action. And, as the people who commissioned our partners to find senior executives knew, this leadership had relevant line experience. It had delivered results before under similar circumstances.

2. These companies were relentless in pursuit of "before-the-fact strategies." They steered by a clear vision of what works in the relevant market. They understood what customers needed, and understood their own strengths and weaknesses, as well as those of their competitors. Their vision was expressed in terms of market dominance, not financial returns. They adhered to simple performance measures. But this relentless pursuit of strategy was not a source of inflexibility. In fact, it gave them the impetus to be agile and responsive in their core business when necessary because their focus on the market and the customers let them understand when a previously successful strategy had stopped working and it was time to do something different.

3. They were energized by an extraordinarily intense performance-driven environment. The leaders established a culture where there was real accountability. Both professional and personal standards were very high. People who worked there described them as good, but not "nice" places to work. By that they meant that the rewards were not in the perks and benefits, but in being part of a winning institution and achieving notable results.

4. These companies had relatively simple structures. The reporting and accountability lines were clear, and the organizational structures reproducible as the company grew. Even as the company expanded geographically or added product lines or services, it cloned its basic elements rather than reorganize into previously unknown forms.

5. The company's successes were based on world-class skills. These companies did many things well, but one world-class skill area was the vital underpinning of their strategy. They understood that, whether it was marketing savvy, a production or merchandising expertise or a quality/cost expertise, they had to spend whatever it took to be not just the best in their industry, but the best in class worldwide. These companies viewed their management process as one of the competitive skills areas. And they worked at it just as strongly as they worked on the other skills. For example, they understood continuous improvement, but applied it to themselves. The management understood it was not exempt from these notions, but, in fact, had to lead by example since its own sustenance of continuous improvement was the most critical aspect of all.

6. These companies were continuously rejuvenated by well-developed people systems. This had nothing to do with the activities of the HR department, but with the fact that the leadership was aware of the performance of key contributors even two and three levels down. Interaction between the levels of management was provided regularly, so that discussions of problems and awareness of significant issues were shared broadly across all levels.

In sum, all these companies had succeeded in attracting leadership with all the key skills—leadership with relevant industry experience and a reputation for results; leadership that thought strategically and could communicate vision; leadership that related well to people and understood that people and their skills are a company's principal advantage.

I don't imply that McKinsey is the only one with the answer. Consulting firms like A. T. Kearney; Bain & Co.; Booz Allen and a variety of academic institutes have done similar work. And they come up with similar analyses. In the end, there are two conclusions. The first is that it is rational for companies to look for and be willing to pay a premium for outstanding management skill. We know that the relationship between above-average management skills and superior results is not coincidental. The second conclusion is that we also know, with a reasonable level of confidence, what exceptional management looks like. Our research for this book makes it clear that the people who recruit executives have a clear profile that matches the theory and research and are behaving rationally when they pursue it.

Chapter 11

The Early Years

Introduction: Checklist for Pre-MBA Students

If you know that you are going to ultimately get an MBA, even if it's likely to be four or more years away, start planning now. There are several reasons to delay: to rejuvenate your bank book, to acquire more work experience, or to ensure that your work experience includes the kind of *meaningful* positions that will get you into a top-ranked school—at which top-ranked employers run recruiting drives.

Focus on the quality of the experience you are getting before you go back to school, not on the dollars. Quality is denoted in three ways. The first is the nature of the company. The company should be big, have a brand name, and be well-recognized for its training program. The second is the nature of the work. Make sure you are performing a job central to the company's purpose. That means being in the technology, production, or sales and marketing side. Being in customer service or an administrative support function doesn't do much. Do something memorable that shows initiative. Get assigned to an important project. Be where the action is. Third is the nature of the additional activities you take on that demonstrate managerial skills. Be a part of the recruiting team, because only people who have good judgment and can sell are allowed to recruit for the company. Be a spokesman for the organization in any kind of setting. Take on jobs where you must write. It doesn't matter whether the output is training manuals, industry analyses or strategic papers. You want to have evidence that you can use in other settings to show writing and communication skills. Start a peer activity group to show that you can network and that people will follow you. Do things outside your job that also build and demonstrate skills and initiatives. Be involved with your alma mater's alumni organization. Do some kind of competitive sports or music or hobby that takes discipline and dedication. Travel, and get some broadening experience, to illustrate that you are open to and accepting of cultural differences. Learn a language or do something that makes it clear you are comfortable in a different culture.

Then select a cluster of schools and be very strategic about applying. Start early and visit the schools, selling yourself, since personal contact makes your application stand out from the others. And, in general, go to the best school you can, but also focus on size. Some people do less well in a large impersonal school. Consider the personality of the school to ensure you'd be a standout. When companies recruit, they focus on students in the top half of the class. So being distinguished and a leader at a good school is better than being an "also ran" at one of the slightly better institutions.

The Immediate Post-MBA Job—Only Three Rules Matter

The quality of your first job is key to establishing a good foundation. It is not likely to be the place at which you'll spend your whole career. Three rules help ensure the quality of that first job.

Never Let the Dollars Drive You

You will excel at only the jobs you enjoy and that are connected to your vision and goals. Doing things only for the money won't help you in the long term. Don't become so anxious to pay off student loans or buy a new car that you take that job that pays best, regardless of the consequences.

FUTURE LEADERS OF INSTITUTIONS GET EARLY EXPOSURE AT THE TOP AND WITH CUSTOMERS

Get experience at the name-brand companies and in jobs that expose you to top-level issues, whether that be senior staff to the president or senior executives, or the planning, corporate development or strategy groups. Gain broad exposure to show versatility. This can also be achieved in consulting and investment banking careers. Be a fly on the wall where people are doing the kind of work that ultimately senior executives perform, which means setting strategy and executing changes in product or marketing directions. *The cliché about working your way up from the bottom is wrong.* Start at the top in size, quality of company, and level of job interaction. *Then* drop down to get line experience and prove you can achieve results on your way back up to the top.

Another key element is to work directly with customers as soon as you can. No other experience gives would-be managers the necessary sense of how competitive the world is and how people choose companies and products. Whether it be sales, customer service, relationship management or serving the distribution channel, there's no substitute for that tangible sense of the interaction between buyer and seller.

WOULD-BE ENTREPRENEURS EXECUTE A ONE-STEP OR TWO-STEP STRATEGY

Don't be afraid to start right away. If you are going to start your own company, there is no better time than right out of school. Either go where the action and learning is, or develop a business plan and see if you can attract money. If you really need to do it in a two-step process, study the successes and go where you can build the contacts or the expertise that are the minimum requirement. There is a lot to be said for building up contacts among prospective customers. The hardest thing to do, even if you have a great idea, is to lock in that initial book of revenue that allows you to be free of people's money. If even on a modest scale you can attract orders, that reduces your day-to-day risk of the twin disasters of the entrepreneur: running out of money, or having to give away too much to investors in the start-up phase. The best two-step plans provide a running start on the revenue side.

When to Hold 'Em; When to Fold 'Em

There will come a time when you have received what you need from job number one. At three to four years out, if you're not continuing to build your skills, it's time for the next step. There's always a price to pay and a risk to take in considering a job move. A successful progression to successively better jobs is difficult enough to achieve, and is particularly difficult to envision at the beginning. In hindsight, what seems to be progression at the time may appear to be an erratic pattern of job hopping. Even if you believe it is time to look around after your first few years, keep several perspectives in mind.

BE PATIENT

A stall or plateau for a person in her late 20s is, in fact, significantly preferable to a flaming crash landing at this career stage. No one expects you to be promoted every 18 to 36 months. But you are expected to exercise good judgment and show maturity and patience in how you balance your need to build a career with your employer's need for you to get things done.

ALWAYS GO *TO SOMETHING*, NOT *AWAY FROM* SOMETHING

I encourage people to use the "two-to-one rule." That is, make sure there are at least *two* good reasons to seek a new job for every one reason you want to get out of your existing job. If you are running away, you probably have blinders on. That's when you start overlooking risks and obstacles. A bad boss, an unfair review, or a disappointment that a colleague seems to receive better treatment doesn't show up on a resume. What does show up is a stupid or impetuous move that you then have to undo or explain many times over the next few years.

FOCUS ON THE POSITIVE AND THE LONG-TERM

Be motivated by long-term gain, not short-term gain. Competitive athletes understand that a bad sprain or a jammed finger heals by itself. They don't asked to be traded or tear up their contract if they're benched temporarily by one of these short-term afflictions. They recognize that it makes no sense to go down to the minor leagues to stay a "starter" during these kind of temporary interruptions. Similarly, putting yourself in a position where you can't use your skills or demonstrate the level at which you can be competitive is much worse than being temporarily sidelined by a frustrating boss or a marginal assignment. Keep thinking of how someone will look at your resume when it's time for you to be considered for a senior executive position. No one will know or even understand that you think that you should have been promoted six or nine months earlier. If your response was to move to a problem company or into a less challenging environment, what they will see is that you couldn't compete in the top tier.

Where Should You Be by Age 30?

All senior executive jobs require the same five to six profile elements. You're better off gaining some of each at every stage than trying to max out on some early and fill in the rest later. For example, some executives might say, "I'll concentrate on getting my line experience early and not worry about developing communication skills or strategic thinking skills until I have at least two or three assignments where I can point to clear results," but that's a strategy that can haunt you. Opportunity comes at odd times and in odd places, so you're better off being ready. In the competition with other executive candidates, being somewhat more experienced or skilled in one dimension doesn't offset having a void in one of the five or six key dimensions; it just takes you out of the running entirely.

HAVE A RECORD FOR BEING A COMPETITOR

This is the precursor to having a reputation for results. At this stage, being able to start building a record will depend to large degree on who selects you. It will be a reflection of schools and firms. It will be demonstrated in what you have achieved in academic, extracurricular and other activities. It will be shown in the nature of the jobs or other work you are doing, i.e., are they pre-managerial? No one expects you to be running a division at age 27. But those who will be evaluating your record in later years and considering you for a position in senior management *do* expect to see a pattern that demonstrates the willingness of other people to invest in you for the long term. Leaders don't emerge from nowhere at age 35.

All this is really saying the same thing. At this stage of your career, you'll be known much more by the company you keep than by your individual accomplishments because they're so hard to calibrate. For example, everyone has a clear image of what it means to be a U.S. Marine or a Green Beret. In fact, it might be much more impressive to say that you were an installation commander in the Coast Guard by the time you were 27, but that takes much more knowledge and insight to appreciate.

SECURE LINE EXPERIENCE IN THE RIGHT INDUSTRY

To be mobile as a manager you must have direct qualifying experience by the time you are 30. You need exposure to both the technology and the techniques of the industry sectors you expect to move in. You must be on the line, in the mainstream, in the right functions, handling mainstream projects such as new products, mergers, reengineering or global expansion. Again, no one expects you to be fully in charge. But you must be doing things that demonstrate you are part of the group that is making the fundamental business decisions.

CONTINUE TO DEMONSTRATE EXECUTIVE SKILLS IN COMMUNICATIONS, INTERPERSONAL RELATIONSHIPS AND STRATEGIC THINKING

To a large degree this is the same advice as for the pre-MBAs. The real trick is to put yourself in a position to allow those skills to develop. If, for example, you're not in a managerial or supervisory position, then you need to get involved in projects or task forces where it's clear that you have something to contribute beyond your personal proficiency in your own discipline. If you are in sales, you should volunteer to put together a sales training program or to write the strategic plan for a new product line or product line extension. If you are in engineering or production, offer to write a "layman's language" overview for new managerial hires of where key technology is heading. If you are in finance, prepare an analysis of the successful and unsuccessful acquisitions of your competitors or in a comparable industry. In all cases, you want to practice your executive skills. You want to demonstrate that you think like senior management, that is, you think beyond your own function or disciplines, and you want to build a reputation for being someone who provides thought leadership and initiative beyond just doing your assigned job well.

START GETTING ON THE RADAR

Remember what we said. It's other people in the industry to whom search consultants turn when they want lists of candidates. Join the industry associations, and don't be reluctant to take the entry-level positions on these committees. No one expects someone in their twenties to be heading industry groups. Build a reputation for being a good worker, reliable, conscientious, and not afraid to roll up your sleeves. As you move up the corporate ladder in your own company, these industry colleagues and acquaintances will assume you're doing your own current work with that same degree of diligence. People who say, "I'm going to maximize my reputation within the company before I 'waste' time on outside activities," are missing a big opportunity. Think about how the wave from a stone dropped in a pond spreads long after the stone has hit the surface. The outer rings of the ripple are still spreading even if you're only making little splashes initially. If you make enough of them and give them enough time to spread, the wave you generate will have reached everywhere in your particular pond.

Chapter 12

Into the Fray

Introduction

The years from the early 30s to the mid–40s are those that shape careers. There is enough time left to recover from false starts, late starts, detours and dead ends. But enough time has passed to have a real record, to have created a distinguishable profile, and to have developed a depth of skill.

This is the age group that can best take advantage of the lessons of the search firm files. This is the group that starts to show up on the short list for division-head jobs, presidential jobs, CEO and chairman positions.

The checklist of qualifications for executives in this age group includes the same things listed in Part Two. These qualifications determine who ends up on the radar and who receives the job offers.

They are also the same things that we discussed in Chapter 5 ("Why a Headhunter Makes You a Candidate"):

- You hold a position in which you demonstrate both accountability and results.

- You have people outside your company who can attest to your influence, character and managerial style.
- You think and communicate at a strategic level.
- You have your ego in check, and good interpersonal skills.
- You have had a series of increasingly responsible line jobs.

Ironically, you are not "career-obsessed." For the most part, you focus on giving to the people you serve—which includes your employees, customers, superiors and shareholders. This is what motivates you. This is what you use to keep score of your progress. But you also keep your eye on whether you are building the kind of well-rounded profile that helps keep options open.

There are, however, a number of questions that arise in the career of most executives in your category. There are certain predictable forks in the road that many of those like you must face. These questions are not avoidable in the sense that making no decision is, in fact, selecting one of the paths. So for executives in this career stage there are a few more questions to be answered over and above whether they are making steady progress on building the right kind of profile.

When Do You Trade a Large, Prestigious Firm for a Smaller One with More Opportunity and Accountability?

Almost every executive on the rise has faced the question of when and if to leave the mother ship. Opportunities to leave middle and upper-middle management jobs at big firms for more senior management jobs at smaller firms are always out there. How do you know if and when it is time to say yes?

The first principle is that it is always easier to go from bigger to smaller than from smaller back to bigger. If your goal is to be a senior manager at a large company, then it is easier if you stay in the large company. It may be inaccurate, or unfair, but the perception is that only people who play in the big leagues can handle big-league pitching. Understand that this is a one-way gate with only a few exceptions.

My advice is to say no to any opportunity with a smaller company if that move would be your first general management line job. I would also recommend that you say no if it is not the kind of job that you think will satisfy your ambitions for five to eight years in terms of opportunity and compensation. The reality is that you will be harder to find, and more typecast, after this kind of move. So to take this kind of job with the expectation you could move on in a year or two is probably not playing the percentages. On the other hand, if you have already had at least two or three line experiences and have established yourself in a big company (that is, you have become a corporate officer or the head of a substantial business unit), then you can make this kind of move with greater freedom. At this stage you have an outside network of references and have established your profile.

Also, if the move is either to the top job or to the position of the heir apparent at a smaller company, you can take it on with a higher sense of confidence. After this kind of move you will have both big company experience and a record of accountability. Under these circumstances you don't need to be as certain that you will find this new job to be the end game in and of itself.

When to Leave the Head Office and Go Overseas

Everyone talks about the value and benefits of having international experience. It's all true. But there is also the reality that careers develop differently when you are out in the field, and you can't be blind to that. As a practical matter there are probably two appropriate times to take an overseas assignment. The first is early in your career. You get your international ticket punched, and you are marked as someone with flexibility, initiative and willingness to take risk. And the nature of the jobs will be such that results—for good or bad—will not be tied directly to you. It may also be a period where the effect on family and social life will be more manageable than it might be in later days.

The flip side of the coin is that it is very important to get back to the company's mainstream during the next phase of your career. Rightly or wrongly, there is a tendency to view people who spend much of their careers moving around overseas as being "permanent expatriates" who are mostly attracted to the glitter and lifestyle of overseas work. Many of today's senior executives remember the 1950s and 1960s when the expatriates were given big salary adjustments to compensate for overseas hardship duties while being provided housing, cars, household help, all the time enjoying the freedom from head office pressure, and a business pace that was somewhere between relaxed and languid. While this reality no longer exists, the stereotype persists.

Another good time go overseas is as you get near the top and have the opportunity to run an international region or product group. At this stage you will be involved in a job where you can demonstrate results, with the added dimension of having achieved them in a different culture. That is an incredibly valuable practical experience as well as a most useful addition to your profile.

When to Take an Assignment That Helps You Learn about Your Weaknesses versus Relying on Your Strengths

You might, for example, know that your principal strengths and aptitudes are marketing and sales. Finance and other quantitative disciplines leave you shuddering. But you know that CEO prospects must understand that side of the business. Some of the rules for gaining this kind of useful broadening are similar to those for international assignments. Get the experience early, or add it late when you can be directly in charge and rely on other people with the technical skills so that your contribution is strategic.

When taking on functions that are not your strong suit, there are two important rules. The first is that you ought to have an "exit ticket" signed by your senior management. By exit ticket I mean a clear understanding that this is an assignment that you are taking on for broadening purposes, and that, within a specified period, you will be moved back into a function that relies on your strengths. The best kind of exit visa is, of course, where the specific assignment to which you will move is agreed upon in advance. Failing that, your agreement ought to be with more then one senior manager, so a turnover or reassignment of one person doesn't void your understanding.

The other rule is *not* to take on this kind of broadening assignment when you suspect that you will need a platform of strength to move on to the next stage. The reality is that, in the eyes of the outside world, you are always typecast in whatever function you currently occupy. If you are a marketing genius who just happens to take a swing through production, many of the things that come your way will be in the production zone. Alternatively, you will be at a disadvantage in competing for marketing jobs since (while in production), you will look like an operations guy trying to make a move into marketing. While inaccurate, this creates a perceived risk that few hiring managers particularly want to take.

Can You Do a Trial Run as an Entrepreneur?

This has the same dimensions as going from a big company to a small company. The passage from corporate-executive-in-the-making to entrepreneur is usually a one-way ticket. There are two reasons for this. First, those who become real entrepreneurs won't ever relinquish the kind of control they have, or the sense of speed and excitement that comes from running your own show, to return to the vagaries of corporate life. And even if they want to, the corporate world has learned from long experience that entrepreneurs are not "housebroken" enough to become satisfied and conforming citizens of a corporate culture.

The second reason it doesn't work is that entrepreneurs don't have the kind of leadership skills that corporate managers need. When you are the owner you move quickly and without consultation. You don't really have a peer group. You develop a "my way or the highway" mentality. You know that speed and responsiveness are your keys to survival. As a result, many entrepreneurs don't develop the ability to visualize and communicate a strategic situation to motivate large groups of colleagues and subordinates. And yet this skill is essential because in the large corporate world these colleagues and subordinates do, in fact, have the option of not following your every command blindly.

So if you're planning to take the big dive off the high cliff and start swimming on your own, realize that entrepreneurs move from one entrepreneurial situation to another but not back and forth to the executive suite.

The experience of H. Ross Perot when his company, EDS, was acquired by GM is probably very instructive. Perot is the ultimate entrepreneur. There was no inclination on his part to change the style that worked when he was the head of his own company. He second-guessed managers who ran business units. He criticized GM's senior officers as lacking vision. And he took his assessments of their shortcomings public. This obviously was a source of profound irritation and discomfort to the directors and managers of a company as large and institutionalized as General Motors. In a high percentage of the cases where an institutionally-managed company acquires an entrepreneurial company, the founder/entrepreneur will end up leaving within 12 to 24 months.

There are some exceptions to this rule. The exceptions typically arise where the managers who have built a business are acquired when an industry is consolidating. The acquiring company usually needs the talent and drive of those "acquired" managers as well as the continuity they contribute to maintain relationships with the acquired organization as well as with the franchise the acquiring company has purchased. Banking is a good example of this. Over the last 15 years there have been a number of cases of managers who have left large banks to head medium-sized or regional groups that were then acquired. These people returned to become part of the senior management team of the acquiring company. But with all due respect to my former profession, the reality is that bankers are not entrepreneurs. Their mind-set is more fiduciary and institutional so these transitions are less difficult.

Can You Afford a Tour in Politics or Government Service?

This is a less common but still relevant question. Higher and higher degrees of interactivity between business and government would suggest that people who have spent time on both sides of that line would be better equipped to handle executive responsibilities. But that is only textbook thinking. The reality is that, like entrepreneurship, the cultures are so different that it is the rare individual who can survive the transition.

To begin with, the vast majority of government jobs are in municipal and state agencies. It is very hard to make a case that experience at either of these levels translates into anything useful for executive careers. The issues in state government do not have much overlap with business. They deal with the delivery of social services, education, the building of roads and the operation of prisons, none of which have private sector transferability.

The person who has already had responsibility as a president or CEO and who can attract a federal cabinet or subcabinet position broadens his profile. But for those who haven't made it to the top job, government service complicates the factors in building an executive career. There are a few exceptions, but they are those that occur early. White House staff service in your late 20s or early 30s would be a positive factor, as would short stints in agency and legislative staff positions in the federal government. It would be even better if you had a line job or two beforehand so that you could reenter the private sector after a few years of government experience. But it is not likely that someone in her mid to late 30s and who is just beginning to crack upper management will do anything except complicate her career planning by taking a government position. This is the time when the "market" is expecting her to be showing that she can deliver clear results for shareholders. You don't do that in government.

What about a Sabbatical?

Despite all the hype about family leaves and multiple sequential careers, the reality in the corporate world is this is very hard to do. There is a persistent belief that "real executives" are maniacally focused on their careers, don't take time off and don't give these kinds of "other issues" much priority. It is not clear whether this mind-set comes from jealousy, from the intensity of the competition, or some sort of residual machismo. But they reality is that it is still there. While it is now diminishing, there is still a double standard that labels women who *are* this career-focused as "libbers" and men who *aren't* as dilettantes.

Among prospective employers it is easier to explain being out of work for nine months because you were fired or downsized than it is to explain that you took off nine months to handle primary child care duties or to give your spouse an opportunity to explore options. Even less acceptable is the notion of taking a year off to "smell the roses," learn Sanskrit, or get in touch with your "inner child."

The Fact That Exceptions to the Profile Are Risky Doesn't Mean They Aren't Valuable and Rewarding

Anything that creates a deviation or exception to the standard profile does, in fact, require one more conversation and one more act of understanding and faith that this exception doesn't detract from your capabilities as an executive. It doesn't mean that these things aren't worth doing. Having a well-rounded executive profile is only one aspect of building an executive career. So the fact that we point out the risks and the trade-offs should be understood only in the context of creating the kind of profile that is most likely to attract outside opportunities. There is much more to life than becoming a CEO, and there are complicated personal issues in terms of development, experience and relationships that all those wishing careers have to consider. In Part Five we will talk about the broader perspective and the prices that people pay for pursuing executive opportunities.

During these critical years there is a clear advantage to developing a certain kind of profile if you want to improve your odds for achieving senior executive jobs. But this profile is not a formula for happiness or for self-esteem. It is what it is. Individuals have to see it as the product of an impersonal marketplace and decide whether the pros and cons make sense for them as individuals in a much broader context.

King of the Hill

Introduction

In this chapter we consider what it is like for you when you're ready to be considered for one of the corporate world's top jobs. You're ready to be a CEO. You are well regarded and well treated where you are, but it may be a long time until the top job opens up. Or you have gone as far as you can because there is an heir apparent or you're a foreign national in a company where "natives" get the top job. But for whatever reason, the stakes are high and the number of opportunities is likely to be relatively small.

You have a number of big questions to ask yourself. How urgent is the need to make a move? You may have no chance for advancement where you are, but the consequences of a wrong decision are even worse. You may feel impatient, but it would be unwise to take the first train out of town. To take a CEO's job where the fit is bad, or the odds for success are low, will only place you into a situation later where all your options are bad, or worse. So pick carefully. The key question is how to ensure that you get to see a reasonable sample and then do the right things once the process starts.

Understand That the List of Openings Is Short

When your next move is to the CEO's chair, you already know half to two-thirds of the companies where that would make sense. At your level, prior industry or analogous experience narrows the field, so you know which ones you are or could be in line for. That means you must keep up-to-date on those companies. You must understand when things are occurring that might create an opportunity. Also, you want to become visible among the directors and other members of the target companies' "official families."

Network with Other CEOs and CEOs to Be

Spread your record and reputation to people who are peers to the job you might want to pursue. When search firms call around, they will look for other CEOs or presidents, both to see if they are interested and to get other names. If you have been involved in civic and community groups at this level, both your style and record will bounce back from these people. Again, this is just your version of the lesson that we talked about earlier, networking with peers. But for CEO level candidates, that peer group is very broad. So you need to break out of trade and industry groups and into leadership-oriented groups. These are likely to be civic, community, and broadly-based professional organizations.

Answer the Three Unavoidable Questions

Once you have begun an active search, in addition to all the rules for getting on the radar, candidates for CEO jobs must be conscious of three key questions. The number of positions is relatively small and their visibility very high. There is always the risk of hurting your current situation by being perceived as being too actively looking, or too publicly disenchanted with your current situation.

Is All Publicity Good?

People have different approaches to this question. Some contend that as long as the relatively small number of the "right" people are aware of you, broader publicity isn't useful and can even hurt. The press is not interested in helping you with your career. The more interesting stories are negative ones, and there is always a risk in trying to attract press coverage for yourself and your accomplishments. On the other hand, it is one of the few ways that a broad audience understands your relative contributions and association with successful events. Most say that there is no easy answer to this question, and it is a function of your own comfort and expertise. It should also be a function of the level of confidence you have in the particular reporter or media. Some are less inclined to find the negative or controversial.

A related question is whether you would want publicity that you are being considered for another CEO job. It can make it clear you're in demand. But it can also suggest you came in second if someone else is selected and you don't publicly decline interest. In general it's always safest to say that you're happy and content to do what you are doing. The people who are looking for talent aren't going to be deterred by that, even if they believe it.

WHO DO YOU TELL THAT YOU ARE LOOKING?

You live in a world where everyone knows everyone. How do you get the word out without it becoming the kind of common knowledge that doesn't advance your cause? Most search firm partners say that, generally, the fewer people you tell, the better. If there are partners at the major search firms whom you trust, you can be somewhat candid. They will understand what you mean anyway, and they are not deterred from talking to people who aren't viewed as being "on the market." In general it is better to take the position that, "I'm always open to conversation, but I am not eagerly trying to change my circumstances." As long as you are visible in a broad sense, whatever situations are out there will find you regardless of whether you advertise interest.

DO YOU EVER QUIT TO CONDUCT A SEARCH FULL-TIME?

The answer is, "It depends." For the most part, there is no great advantage in stepping away from a job to conduct a search. Even if all of the reasons are good, it raises questions. The exceptions might be a merger, for example, where you clearly are odd man out. It also might be warranted when the company you are with is headed to a disaster you can't prevent, or when a major disagreement between you and the board is headed for a public explosion. But most people feel that you should quit altogether only when it is the substantially lesser of two evils.

Is There a Director in the House?

Another part of the senior management career game is to determine whether you want to pursue outside directorships. These can be a source of great education, networking, and experiences that you can't get within your own company. But they also take time and energy. While director compensation is improving, on a per-hour basis it doesn't hold a candle to what you will earn as a senior executive in your own company. So decide how much time you can afford to spend away from your primary business.

WHICH IS THE CHICKEN AND WHICH IS THE EGG?

People say, "Well, how do I get to be a director?" The honest answer is, "Figure out how to get to be the CEO or an inside director of a company and then director opportunities will come to you." People want other CEOs on their board. Various shareholder groups and shareholder representative groups are pushing companies to populate their boards with outside CEOs both for the experience and the accountability.

HOW MANY IS TOO MANY?

There are points of both diminishing returns and outright negative returns if you put too much time and effort into outside directorships. Since the payoff is in contacts, experience and exposure, not in money, you have to ask yourself at what point you have covered the waterfront. In general you are better off being on fewer boards, but on those with more broadly-based and more recognizable companies. The networking value will be better and the peer group higher. Serving on one or two well-established, well-recognized companies with national boards is better than serving on three or four lesser companies. The challenge is deciding which ones you should pass up because it is the smaller ones that are offered earlier in your career.

Being a Good Director

You are invited to serve on boards partly because you earned a reputation as being a good director. A good director has three traits. First, she does her homework. She learns enough to be informed and focused on the right questions and makes good use of the information the company provides, but doesn't expect to be spoon-fed. She doesn't waste time asking questions that are easily answered by reading the package. Second, she uses her contacts to promote the firm. While the director's role is in governance, directors who take a "sit back, fold my arms, I'm here to judge you" attitude won't be invited to serve on other boards. The director should help to sell product, recruit people, and help the company build new relationships. Third, she doesn't showboat. Her job is to help the CEO do his job as well as she can. If she has a criticism or suggestion for improvement it ought to be made in private, at least the first time. The director gives the CEO the chance to get the benefit of her counsel. A director who takes her shots in public will not only make the CEO defensive, but will also create a reputation as being more interested in scoring points then getting results.

ONLY TAKE DIRECTORSHIPS THAT YOU PLAN TO STAY WITH FOR THE LONG HAUL

It is considered bad form to accept a directorship and then resign within a couple of years, especially if it is for a better offer. A director resigning or not standing for reelection tends to be viewed by the market as a signal of something amiss and certainly invites inquiries. In general, if you can't serve for at least five or six years, then you probably shouldn't accept an offer.

SHOW THE SKILLS OF A GOOD CEO TO OTHER DIRECTORS

Board members are people asked about CEO candidates. You want to show the same skills, recognizing that you are not competing with your own CEO. You ask strategic questions, do your homework, display good communication skills. Your questions are cogent, and you are focused and sensitive to other peoples' feelings. You are not arrogant, and you bring forward your own relevant experiences so your reputation for results is gradually communicated.

Being a director is difficult and demanding. That is why companies want to find the most qualified and senior people to serve. It is not something to be treated as a perk or benefit. It is an investment in the company on whose board you serve, in their management and on behalf of their shareholders. It requires time and energy, and creates risk and obligations. There are benefits in networking and experience. On balance, you should believe in the company and limit the number of directorships you attempt. Directorships are opportunities to serve and learn as well as opportunities to be seen and become visible. But it is hard to do them well. If you try to do more than just a few, you will almost certainly neglect something for which you are more directly responsible.

PART FIVE

Keeping It in Perspective

Building an executive profile is not cost free. In fact, there are some fairly high prices to pay. You lose spontaneity about and control over the range of experiences you might want to enjoy. You must have a high tolerance for frustration and the ability to adopt a longer-term agenda with patience. You must understand and manage consequences for your spouse and family.

In these last two chapters we will expand on this theme of trade-offs. In a book full of advice on how to get to become a senior executive, it may be assumed that you *must* become a senior executive:

- If you want to be happy
- If you want to be fulfilled
- If you want to be a success
- If you want to be a good person
- If you want to get the most out of life

But there are two realities to think about regularly so you don't fall into this trap. The first is that most people aren't senior executives and many of them are content. The other is that, of the ones who are top executives, no higher percentage of them feel happy and fulfilled than you would find among the rest of the population. The first corollary is there is much randomness involved in who gets these kinds of positions. With a game involving this much chance, don't use your success or lack of it in any meaningful way as a measure of yourself and your worthiness as a person. In fact, it is probably no more realistic to tie your sense of self-worth to this game than it would be to your ability to win at blackjack. Blackjack is fun to play; it can be rewarding; it does take skill but the odds are stacked against the player. In that way the analogy holds.

Chapter 14

Skill and Chance at Work

Understand the Odds

When you look at the numbers involved in executive careers, the message you should take away is *not* that you can't do it if you want to. You can. The message to understand is this: If you take this as a measure of your merit, you don't fully understand the numbers.

Obviously there are a thousand CEOs in the Fortune 1000. And there are only another 15,000 or so companies that have listed securities, which indicates a public company in any practical sense of the word. Let's presume the top 30 jobs in any Fortune 1000 company constitute "executive" management. That's generous. Then for the 15,000 other companies, we'll call at most the top five jobs "executive" management. The sum of those two gives you only slightly over 100,000 "top" management jobs in this country. There are 75–100 million adults in the age range that would, at least theoretically, qualify them for management positions. So we are talking about a profession that one-tenth of one percent of the population could pursue and expect to reach the top of. There are obviously many more people who are, in fact, in management jobs, and doing useful things. But if you define success only if you get to one of those top jobs, you play a game with some long odds against you.

Understanding the Odds and the Timing Issues

Another way of understanding the role of randomness in executive careers is to imagine all the things that must occur simultaneously for you to start the process of capturing an opportunity outside your own company.

The following events have to happen simultaneously:

1. You have to be looking for another opportunity.
2. You have to have the elements of a profile that will attract a search firm.
3. Another company has to need someone with your profile and that company has to conclude there are no internal candidates.
4. That company has to decide to put that position out for executive search.
5. They have to pick a search firm that is one of the few that has some likelihood of coming across you.
6. The search firm has to find you and decide that you are one of the ten or fifteen people who they should profile to the employer.
7. You have to be one of the four to six people that the search firm presents as a semifinalist.
8. You have to beat out the other three to five candidates whom the company interviews directly.

Mathematics shows you how much randomness occurs. Because these are not totally independent events, the math isn't particularly pure. But even if each of these events has a one in ten chance of happening at a particular time relevant for you, the joint probability that they all happen simultaneously so that you end up being the winning candidate is less than one in ten million. So how do you approach this and still keep your perspective and optimism?

A Watched Pot Never Boils

So if the odds are so low and the randomness so high, what do you do? Isn't that a formula for frustration? The best advice is to do what great athletes do. Michael Jordan says that he plays his best game when he "lets the game come to him." In other words, keep doing things you know how to do well and assume that they will work, as opposed to pressing for a specific outcome. Great golfers say the same thing. Don't worry about your score and the competition, but "get into the moment" and "feel" your swing and enjoy the flight of each ball. Think about each shot and don't get ahead of yourself.

Also, study what a good fisherman knows. That is, keep fishing where you know there is good fishing and ultimately the fish will bite. On a particular day there might not be any fish. But don't start jumping around. Stay with the high odds. For any one fish, or for any one executive job, your odds may be a fraction of a percent. But over a reasonable period, the odds are that a few of them are going to land at your doorstep.

Another piece of advice, especially if you are feeling it is time to move, is to keep your passion level high. If you have no passion for your current job, then get into a volunteer activity or civic group. Do something that energizes you, and makes you feel like you are doing something worthwhile. You'll meet a different set of contacts and feel like you are not just biding your time. In fact, broadening your participation in these kinds of indirect ventures and nonjob activities will generate more opportunity than if you go out and press hard.

Finally, there is the role of "positive intent." You understand the rules; you understand the profile. Now, if it is really that important to you, you have to commit yourself. While Scott Adams, the cartoonist and author of Dilbert, was still working in a corporate job and trying to build a career as a cartoonist, he would write down ten times every day, "I will be the greatest cartoonist in the world." All studies of successful people include a reference to this deliberate intent. Write your ambition down every day. Update "to-do" lists weekly that include doing at least one thing to enhance each of the four or five key parts of your executive profile or your network. Don't daydream, but visualize with intent and commitment.

You Need Help to Measure Your Own Height

The other component of making things happen is to get an honest read on why things are not coming your way. Or assess why the kind of things coming your way don't fit you or your goals.

These are two separate issues. There may be opportunities where the fit is bad. (The smart executive doesn't take those things just because they seem somewhat better. She knows that there is a particular kind of job in a particular kind of environment that she will enjoy and at which she will do well.) But there may be situations where it is the right kind of job, the fit looks good and either you're not being offered the opportunity to be a candidate or you're not making it past the first round. Trying to understand how the outside world sees your profile and skills is a very difficult thing to do. Your friends and colleagues can't be a practical or useful source of constructive input. Asking colleagues has its risks; friends will give you sugarcoated versions out of consideration for your feelings.

Search firms are not in business to give you feedback and are not likely to want to judge or discourage someone. While there may be the exceptional partner with whom you have the kind of relationship that allows you to get candid feedback, consider actually buying some time from one of the outplacement firms even when you don't need outplacement. This can be a practical way of getting an "outside-in" look. The firm can help you do an inventory of skills and a catalog of interests. It may be that your interests are, in fact, in an area different from your preconception of what you think you "ought" to pursue. The firm can also look at your resume and tell you how it will be perceived from the outside. They can tell you where, if you were in an outplacement mode, you should target the job search, and the kind of jobs for which you would be seen as eligible. This feedback can be useful in calibrating your expectations.

Again, like networking, this kind of activity is best done when there is no urgency or pressure. However, surprisingly few people get an independent, third-party opinion on their career.

Chapter 15

Promotions
Aren't Happiness

Chasing Our Myths

The way I was raised matched, in almost every respect, the most typical profile of people who become CEOs. I didn't do it by design. But as I have studied the research done on this topic, a remarkably high percentage of CEOs have these elements in their background:

1. They came from a middle-class family with a manager/professional father and a stay-at-home mother.

2. They were the oldest or only male child.

3. They went to a traditional school that emphasized reading, writing and logical thinking, and were both disciplined and self-disciplined. In many cases they attended church-affiliated schools (for example, a statistically exceptional percentage of corporate CEOs, especially in banking, were educated by the Jesuits).

4. They attended a liberal arts college in the East, took some economics courses and had reasonable exposure to math and

the physical sciences. They were a student leader while in college. They went to one of the top MBA programs. And they started in an executive development program with one of the national brand-name firms committed to management training.

It never occurred to me that someday I wouldn't run something. Even worse, I assumed that if it didn't happen, it would have been some kind of failure on my part. That is still a myth I can't totally shake. But over the years, as I have understood the role of randomness, the myth doesn't have quite as pernicious a hold on me. Confronting this myth helps me see that there are other ways to be of service and feel that you have made useful work of your life. That is the point of the essay included at the end of this chapter.

But there are two other myths that managers on the rise often hold. As these managers mature, they usually learn these myths are false.

Myth One: It Gets Easier at the Top

This is an understandable belief. You look at the CEO and see that he has subordinates who handle the mail, book appointments, and provide chauffeur services. In terms of the hassles of daily life, it appears that CEOs have an easy ride. The reality is that the reason other people do all of those things is that your time is totally consumed by other activities that are even more demanding and certainly more stressful. You have the responsibility for peoples' lives and money. You are required to act quickly with less than full information on developments that might take months or years to unfold.

The parallel myth is that if you are a good manager, eventually run themselves. While the "it gets easier" myth attracts people on the way up, a more dangerous trap awaits the manager who believes that, with the right kind of process, structure and incentive systems, he can make his company a perpetual motion machine. From then on, duties will be handled automatically and than he is free to become a "statesman."

The creation of this myth is an understandable human phenomenon. You have said the same things so many times that you expect that even people new to the company should understand them. So you spend less time communicating. After the twentieth year of quarterly budget reviews, they lose their appeal. So you do fewer of them or delegate them to someone else. Or, since you visited all the plants and the big customers three years ago, there's no need to do that over and over again. But you *have* to do it just as well, and with just as much energy, the thirty-fourth time as you did it the first time. If you don't, things start to unwind. That is why many senior executives finally realize there is a finite amount of time that you can do the same job before you run out of ideas, or energy, or willingness to do things with the same intensity. You need to be "repotted" or return to a lower point on the learning curve to reestablish the sense of novelty that goes with doing the job as well as you can.

Myth Two: Life Is Better at the Top

I would never denigrate the advantages of an executive career. Financially you have great flexibility. There's enormous opportunity for the development of your skills. There is a satisfaction that comes from the sense of control and influence that few professions can match. There is variety, an opportunity to learn about the world, to deal with interesting people, and be spared many of the irritations and frustrations of day-to-day life. But having said all that, it is not necessarily a better life. Many executives assume that *all* good things come as they move up to the top. That thinking sets themselves up for a bad fall.

As you earn more money, the reality is you won't have the time to spend it. You spend money to "buy" free time, but time will still be in short supply. You will have more prestige, but that is not the same as respect or affection. Those come from your character, not the job you hold. The position will attract people, and you'll have lots of contact with others. People are nice to you, so it is easy to assume that you have many friends. But those relationships are colored by your ability to affect other peoples' lives. There is nothing inherently wrong with these kind of contacts, and they are enjoyable. But you need a healthy understanding of the one-dimensional nature of such relationships.

At the end of a book on executive careers it may seem funny to have the author tell you that the top is not all that it's cracked up to be. I am not saying that it is bad, or unpleasant, or not worth pursuing. There are many, many advantages. Your time and effort in becoming an effective manager will be both satisfying and worthwhile. My point is only that it doesn't automatically bring the other dimensions of a satisfying and well-rounded life. There's a tendency both among people on the way up and those already there to assume that success in the business world automatically brings the rest of life's good things. And while it's not true, the real problem with this thinking is that it then makes you terribly nervous about ever losing that executive job because you begin to believe that everything good in life is tied to it. The good news is that since the job doesn't bring all the important things along with it, it can't then carry them away. That is a very hard reality to embrace. Which is why I wrote the essay which is the last section of this chapter. It may also be why so many people called or wrote to say it either helped them or that it was something they found very useful in bringing up this subject with someone else that they loved and saw as being trapped by their fear of failing.

On Top of the World—and Afraid to Fall*

You are at 25,000 feet, descending into yet another city where people are waiting for you. There are important things to do. You are a senior executive and have risen higher and achieved more than you even dreamed of 20 years ago. Your income is so high that you mentally round it out to the nearest $100,000. As another year begins, you look ahead and conclude that you ought to feel that you are on top of the world, except for one thing: you're scared to death.

Success is not what you thought it would be. It is not a cradle or a hideaway. It is a cage, suspended from the ceiling by the thinnest of threads.

Welcome to the club.

Regardless of how high you are in the corporation and how much power you possess, you can lose it overnight. Just as tension spoils the golf swing, the fear of losing your job becomes paralyzing and makes the loss more likely.

Fortunately, there are a few relatively straightforward ways to eliminate this fear. The fact is that failure is not fatal, but most of us can't picture ourselves outside of our current comfort zone. Here are three exercises to relax the tension and reduce the fear:

---

* John Rau, "On Top of the World—and Afraid to Fall," *The Wall Street Journal,* January 8, 1996. Reprinted with permission of *The Wall Street Journal.* ©1996 Dow Jones & Company, Inc. All rights reserved.

GET PAID AT LEAST ONCE FOR A SKILL OR HOBBY

It's easy to feel trapped by the job market and worry about how you would ever find something else that pays, especially with all those other people out there. The reality is that we all have marketable skills such as writing, speaking, consulting, or designing and selling things. It is how we "package" these with fixed expectations in a single administrative role at just one company that makes us less digestible by the traditional job market.

So identify the skills you could turn to over the next six months. Make an effort to get at least one client for your services. It is important that you get paid; psychologically, when you have done it once, you believe you can do it again. You can always tell the client that you are doing this to give the money to charity if he wonders why you are insisting on payment.

LIVE WAY BELOW YOUR INCOME FOR THREE WEEKS

I'm talking about 20–25 percent of your current standard of living, excluding housing. Obviously you cannot sell the house as part of this experiment, but in every other aspect, budget and live that way. What most people find is that the big expenses that have to be cut are the ones that you took on to prove to other people that you could afford them, not the ones that give you any particular pleasure.

DO A FULL-SCALE LIQUIDATION DRILL

On paper, liquidate everything you own—house, car, gadgets, investments. Call a real estate agent in a town with a major university where you would like to live. Find out what it would take to rent a good townhouse (here in Bloomington, Indiana, the most luxurious three-bedroom townhouse is $825 a month). Apply 40 percent of your assets to living costs. Calculate how many years you could live with the other 60 percent buying an acceptable lifestyle in a vibrant community.

These exercises will convince you that being trapped by the money is mostly in your head. But then you'll say, "It's not just the money. What will I do; who will I be?"

We are programmed to achieve, to please others. We're convinced that the external symbols of success are what bring satisfaction and draw people to us. We have seen people who were the center of the crowd one day only to be shunned six months later because they lost their jobs or suffered major reversals. This identity fear is also the central issue I see working with executives contemplating merging or selling their companies, or facing an executive succession. Here the visualization and experimenting exercises take a little more effort. But those who can visualize alternatives generally handle these transitions more successfully. Here are the drills:

SPEND TIME WITH A COUPLE OF PEOPLE WHO PURSUE SATISFACTION BY CONSTANTLY CHANGING THEIR POSSESSIONS AND STATUS SYMBOLS

Find a person on his or her third trophy spouse. Pick out the one whose cars and houses must always be upgraded. Try to pin down the ones who cannot sit still because there is always another exotic place to be. How do they make you feel? Ask yourself whether this is how you would like your son or daughter to be when he or she grows up.

Ask your spouse and kids to list the things that they like about you, and how they would improve your relationship with them. You'll find they won't mention your job or talk about money. They'll talk about being a partner, knowing more of what is going on with you, having more time, feeling more loved, and seeing you more happy and relaxed. Keep their lists and read them whenever you feel anxious.

WRITE YOUR OBITUARY

Make it long, what you hope your mother, father and your favorite teacher would like to read. Think about when you are gone and what you would like the obituary to say, not what it would say today given the trend line you are on. If you are like most people, you will tear up the first draft because it will be about accomplishments, successes and positions in organizations. You'll realize you want it to be about character, doing useful things, being a good partner and exceptional friend. Put a copy in your locked desk drawer and another in the secret compartment of your briefcase. Read it every morning, and whenever that trapped feeling hits.

Obviously, you do not need to quit your job because of these fears. In fact, doing these exercises to deal with the fear will result in your doing the job even better and enjoying it more. Seneca, the Roman philosopher, said, "You would teach me how I may hold my own and keep my estate; but I would rather learn how I may lose it all and yet be contented." Lily Tomlin put it more succinctly: "The trouble with the rat race is, even if you win it, you are still a rat." The trap is believing that your life is only your career. The solution is just a simple change of perspective. Understand that your career should be living your life your way. Be comforted that the world cannot take away anything from you unless you give the world the power by making those external things your only source of satisfaction.

Chapter 16

Afterwards

Will the Primary Requirements Change?

This book is based on a current snapshot of requirements and expectations for candidates for senior executive positions. It is also a snapshot of positions filled mostly by people between ages 35 and 55, meaning, in this case, people born between 1940 and 1960. So it is fair to ask whether, as time passes, these requirements will be the same.

The top five requirements are essentially timeless skills and transcend specific technologies or industries. The principal requirements for executive success will remain the same over time. These are skills that allow people to deal with increasing change, and with increasing diversity in the workforce, among their customers and among the constituents with whom they interact. It's hard to imagine how any of these will become less important.

I believe that interpersonal and communication skills will be even more important in the future, and the requirement that people have a record of results in the same industry or something nearby will decrease. The moves of executives like Lou Gerstner from RJR to IBM, and Randy Tobias from AT&T to Lilly, all say that in today's world it's the skills of the individual and the ability to master change, create vision, and provide leadership that are more important than the technology/experience base.

Relevant experience will be defined less by industry and more by the kind of issues the company is expected to face. The principal specification will increasingly include having dealt with the kind of change a company must face and less that it include "comparable" industry experience. Clients will increasingly say they want executives from the kind of culture that they want to become.

The principal requirements for executive success will not either change all that much or go out of style. What will change is the kind of preliminary experiences and prequalifying backgrounds that rising managers will have.

The New Qualifying Standards

We talked a little bit about this in Chapter 11, "The Early Years." Unlike the executives who won the competitions included in our sample, if we were to do this book again in 15 or 20 years, I suspect we would find that every successful candidate was also:

- Computer literate, both in the sense of knowing how to use computers as a communication and research tool for herself, as well as understanding how they become a distribution device for products and services.

- Appreciative of how to deal with generations that have moved to a visual and symbolic form of information processing, and away from a logic, narrative and alphabetized form; this generation will process images directly, whereas today's executives turn phonetic symbols first into words and then back into pictures and images.

- Comfortable in dealing with the reality of nonsequential careers for themselves and most of the people within their organizations.

The Global Mind-Set

The other element of the personal portfolio every future manager will need is a comfort with the international mind-set that one must bring to products, competition and opportunities. In practice this means three things:

1. You view your home country as nothing more than one region in a global marketplace. You perceive no barriers or protection to products or capital flows either trying to get in or trying to get out.

2. You understand how cultural differences are a key element in all business plans and organizations. You view cultures as neither good nor evil, only different.

3. You recognize that historical or regional advantages are anomalies. You understand that there is no divine right or guarantee of opportunities or protections for your "natural" market. You organize and manage with this dynamic. You discard the mind-set of trying to extend or perpetuate what were abnormal blips in the long history of commerce.

Industries of the Future

In addition to the global mind-set, future executives must have a working understanding of the six technologies that will produce much of the growth and most of the value in the twenty-first century. Traditional manufacturing and service businesses will increasingly be made commodities by global competition. The availability of labor and capital pools that were walled off just a few years ago behind trade barriers or totalitarian politics has created a surplus of supply for the production of mature products and services. The industries of the future are those that will allow companies to break out of the trap of commodity prices for goods and instant competition from low-cost, global labor. These are the industries that will apply intelligence to create an advantage over low cost and low price. The managers of the future must understand the following industries:

1. **Digital Communications.** This is the "mother" of all technologies. It is the rapid advance in the cost performance curves of communication technologies that will allow the breakthroughs in other sectors. Managers must understand the fundamental notion of how the substitution of information for engineering technology or time and place limits will transform the nature of competitive advantage. They should also understand the fundamental issues of how bandwidth translates into the ability to effectively move high volumes of information and the likely developments in the cost performance curves of the underlying technology. For at least their own industry, they should understand the bandwidth requirements of the key applications and how that compares with distribution technologies already in place.

2. **Robotics.** Robotics is the "working" end of putting digital technologies into the production process. The only way that the industrialized world can compete with the newly liberated labor forces of China and the formerly totalitarian economies of eastern Europe and Latin America will be to offset the huge discrepancies in unit labor cost with the application of technologies. Robotics will permit some companies to use advanced intelligence as a way to compete with more expensive labor and still maintain an overall cost, quality and consistency advantage.

3. **New Materials and Ceramics.** Both deal with the fundamental problem of breaking out of conventional design trade-offs. Speeds, temperatures and pressures are becoming higher and higher in modern applications of all kinds. New forms of ceramics, plastics and nonferrous materials will be the solution to provide the necessary higher tolerances that will accompany these new high-performing products. Similarly, as the environmental and supply trade-offs of traditional materials become clearer and clearer, materials that are environmentally friendly on the disposition side or are totally renewable in terms of resources will become an increasingly important part of a satisfactory and environmentally friendly industrial base.

4. **Computers and Software.** Computers and software are the tools of this age. More and more they will be the basic tools of managers at all levels. Increasingly user-friendly software will allow managers to leverage their intelligence in the analytical and decision-making professions. Being computer literate will be mandatory. As the computer becomes an everyday appliance attached to broadbase networks, the rethinking of the service, retail and distribution businesses will be inevitable.

5. **Civilian Transportation.** Civilian transportation will hold a key position among the six new important industries. This will occur as more of the world's population grows richer. The ability to move people to and from work and to places of service delivery, entertainment and tourism becomes an increasingly important ingredient. As information technology removes the constraints on matching consumers with products, the ability to deliver people and goods anywhere in the world grows more significant. This sector includes everything from environmentally friendly automobiles, mass transit, light and intercity rail, to new forms of high-speed, intercontinental transportation.

6. **Biotech and Bioagriculture/Forestry.** The last major growth industry that managers need to understand will be the biotech animal husbandry and agriculture/forestry sectors. In both cases this will be a movement from chemically-based technologies to more "natural" biologically-based ones. Our current agricultural industry is heavily petroleum-based in terms of the energy needed for cultivation, hydration and pesticides. The cost and environmental consequences of this kind of economy are no longer acceptable. Companies that can provide biologically-based alternatives, lower in energy consumption and toxicity, create major advantages for an economy where farming must be done in smaller and smaller areas closer to watersheds and cities. Similarly, a biotech industry that requires less dependence on pharmaceuticals and surgical procedures and expensive diagnostics will create exceptional value to a society hard pressed to pay for rising health care costs.

In the long-term, "balance-of-payment" sense, consumer societies will pay for the value added by these technologies. Only the countries that can master these knowledge industries will earn an advantage in their own standard of living.

Invest for Retirement Every Day

Successful executives of the future will know that no single company will provide for their financial security. They will understand that they must also provide their own emotional security and provide and prepare for the possibility of several retirements at a variety of stages. There will no longer be a standard retirement age. We will evolve to where some people will retire in their 40s or go to working half-time, or drop back and then "un-retire" later on. Others will continue to work well beyond normal ages. The people with the healthiest attitudes will see retirement, semiretirement or partial retirement as just more challenges and adventures rather than as forms of exile from which there is no return.

What does it take for a person to feel comfortable stepping out of a structured job even for an interim period? Or making a variety of corporate transitions and viewing retirement as positive? The people who successfully master this kind of transition several times in a career will be those who have a variety of other things going on in their life. Like networking, they will have started to do them long before it was necessary.

These "successful" retirees-to-be will have:

- *Hobbies.* They will have things that they feel a passion for, and where they can exert mastery. For them, the enjoyment is the process and the improving, rather than in reaching a specific goal. It is this phenomenon that explains much of the attraction both of golf and gardening.

- *Service.* People eventually discover that living only for yourself makes everything else feel hollow. People involved in meaningful service find satisfaction in the giving.

- *Nonwork relationships.* Successful would-be retirees maintain ties with family and friends outside of the workplace and to people with common interests. They make sure that a meaningful percentage of their relationships are not colored by their corporate status.

- *Curiosity.* It can be the 100 things that you want to do before you die. It can be travel. It can be sciences, or reading, drama or art. Healthy preretirees have things that they will always want to learn more about and feel a sense of exploration and adventure as they pursue.

- *Continued skill building.* Healthy preretirees are those who view themselves as a work in progress. They understand the joy of improving their own skills, whether in sports, music, performance art, writing, speaking, counseling or writing diaries. One of my successful executive friends said that it is hard to feel bad about getting older if there are some things at which you are getting better.

Are Exceptional CEOs and General Managers Worth the Money?

Much has been written lately about the escalation in executive compensation. One can approach this issue from the point of view of societal values and signals. But the debate ought to be informed by an understanding of the economics. If current levels of executive compensation "make sense" in terms of adding value to shareholders, then that colors the issue in a different way than if, in fact, no rational economic case can be made. It is hard to ignore the fact that superior leadership can generate a return far in excess of its costs.

Let's take a company with $800 million in sales, a market value of $500 million and a book equity of $300 million, earning 5 percent on sales or about 13 percent on equity and 8 percent on market capitalization. This is a respectable-sized company, but not one that would make even the antechamber of the Fortune 500. Then let's further presume that we replace the CEO with someone who can drive the margin on sales from 5 percent to 8 percent, increasing the net income from $40 million to $64 million a year. The new CEO has added $24 million a year after tax to the firm's income stream and added several hundred million dollars to its market capitalization. Would you pay $1 million or $2 million more to get this superior CEO? Of course you would. And it would be economically rational to do so.

The furor, of course, should not be over whether the exceptional CEO is worth the compensation. It *is* worth debating whether we are

moving toward a system where even the average or below–average person receives high–performer compensation. That is the more significant and worrisome factor. The reality is that a general manager who
can be 25 percent or 30 percent better than the average will always be
worth substantially more than he or she is paid.

This is the supply side of the question. Rational buyers would clearly
bid up that small number of superior CEOs until their cost equals the
marginal benefit that they can bring to a company's earnings. But it
is clear that in companies of almost every size, we are a long way from
this. So the fact that the compensation levels are lower than what the
market would ultimately pay must have to do with the fact that there
is plenty of supply. There are two factors at work. The first is that there
are many personal benefits from a managerial career—prestige, control,
higher degrees of security, challenge, personal skill development. All of
these encourage people to pursue these careers.

And, certainly in the early stages, it takes less money to attract people to these jobs. Because it is so hard to tell whether the manager you
are considering is one of the superior ones or just average, the excess supply allows the market to say, in effect, "Show me." For the relatively few
where the evidence is clear that they are capable of generating high value
added, the dynamics turn from a buyers' to a sellers' market. The exceptional compensation of the handful of movie stars who are in short supply draws an endless parade of would-be stars into the lower ranks of the
career chain. There will always be managers and executives striving for
the opportunity to prove themselves and become one of those stars.

It seems clear that the market for executives is still stacked in favor
of the buyers, compared with other markets for talent with high economic value. In a typical Fortune 1000 company, the executive management group might have a total cost to the company of less than 2
percent of the firm's income and an effective share of the incremen-
tal income that they earn above a normal rate of return of less than 6
percent or 7 percent There are many industries where this kind of percentage looks meager. In professional sports, the athletes' share of the
total revenue stream might be 60 percent and five to eight times the
level of the owner's profit. Book authors get 12 percent to 15 percent
of the gross revenue which is often 50 percent to 150 percent of the
profit. Commissioned salespeople in many fields are compensated at 10
percent to more than 20 percent of total volume, regardless of whether

the shareholders make money. Total compensation for the sales force often exceeds the total profit for the enterprise. There are also many fields where the compensation to the principals is both higher in total and as a fraction of income than that of business leaders. Any banker will tell you that the people who get rich are not the corporate executives, but the entrepreneurs who start their own firms and whose compensation includes the growth in the total value of the enterprise over time.

Similarly, the people who manage money—venture capitalists, investment bankers or hedge fund operators—generate compensation in a whole other league from that of corporate executives. Look at the list of the top 100 wealthiest people. You will see few, if any, corporate executives; rather, company founders like Bill Gates of Microsoft, and investors like Warren Buffet, the partners of Solomon Brothers and Goldman, Sachs; buy-out artists like Ron Pearlman, and hedge fund operators like George Soros. Perhaps the reason that there is less hue and cry over the compensation of these individuals is that the link between their efforts, whether they be entertainers, sports figures, entrepreneurs or money managers, seems more direct. With corporate officers the connection seems vaguer. It may be easier to assume that either anyone can do it, or that the results happen on their own. So in addition to answering the question, does it make sense to pay high-performing executives well, it also is important to answer the question, do high-performing companies, in fact, result from exceptional executive leadership?

The Last Equation

Society needs good leadership and good leadership will always be in short supply. Much of this book has been focused on how tough the competition is for executive jobs. How, except for a fortunate few, the market favors the buyers of managerial talent. We've discussed the low odds of success in managerial careers and the many things that have to be done right to move up the corporate ladder.

But none of this changes the even more important fact that no society can be any better than the quality of its leadership. Almost every aspect of a society's quality of life depends on how good its leaders are. That is never more true than today. We have global competition and no trade or tariff barriers to hide behind. We have no transportation barriers, and the explosion of technology allows new products to overtake the old in a matter of months. So a firm's ability to prosper will increasingly be a function of its leadership. For our society, the quality of life, standard of living and the opportunities for freedom and personal development depend ultimately on the supply of leadership available.

The good news for us is that there will be a lot more variety in the kind of leadership profiles available. Many talented people who, in times past, might have been excluded from contributing their talents to this common pool will now find that only performance matters.

We increasingly see age stereotypes broken. People who previously might be thought to be too young are taking positions of responsibility. An entrepreneurial market lets the reaction to products rather than someone's tenure or seniority dictate their impact. Similarly, advances in health care and life sciences and the increased focus on preventative fitness means that older people will also be viewed as being able to make contributions as long as they are mentally fit and willing to do so. The executive suite is also open to people with more variety of backgrounds. Social class and educational pedigree are less important in today's meritocracy. And some, but certainly not all, of the barriers that people of color, women and those of diverse ethnic backgrounds have faced are receding.

But the fundamental issues will still be the same, even though we will have a more diverse labor pool to draw from. The competition will push the standard up for everyone. The leaders will be those who have developed their skills, who have taken the long view and focused on getting results, created value for their shareholders and constituencies; who have worked hard, who have worked smart and who have worked patiently.

But, most important, leaders will come from that group of people who bring real enthusiasm to leading people. They will be those who enjoy this often messy, often frustrating, often painful process. They will be the ones who will realize it is a *privilege* to lead people. It is a test of your own humanity to interact with people in all of their human dimensions. For those who have the passion and have the skill, there is a joy to it that no other profession can match. And that, perhaps, is the most important secret of all from the search firm files.

INDEX